# SHARIAH

*A Divine Code of Life*

# SHARIAH

## A Divine Code of Life

*By*

ABDUR RASHID SIDDIQUI

THE ISLAMIC FOUNDATION

*Shariah: a Divine Code of Life*

*Published by*
THE ISLAMIC FOUNDATION,
Markfield Conference Centre, Ratby Lane,
Markfield, Leicestershire LE67 9SY, United Kingdom
E-mail: publications@islamic-foundation.com
Website: www.islamic-foundation.com

Quran House, PO Box 30611, Nairobi, Kenya

PMB 3193, Kano, Nigeria

*Distributed by*: Kube Publishing Ltd.
Tel: +44(01530) 249230, Fax: +44(01530) 249656
E-mail: info@kubepublishing.com



*British Library Cataloguing-in-Publication Data*
A catalogue record for this book is available from the British Library

ISBN: 978-0-86037-624-8 PB
ISBM: 978-0-86037-629-3 e-Book

*Typeset by:* N.A. Qaddoura
*Cover design by:* Nasir Cadir

# CONTENTS

# TRANSLITERATION TABLE

*Arabic Consonants*

Initial, unexpressed medial and final: ء ’

| | | | | | | | |
|---|---|---|---|---|---|---|---|
| ا | a | د | d | ض | ḍ | ك | k |
| ب | b | ذ | dh | ط | ṭ | ل | l |
| ت | t | ر | r | ظ | ẓ | م | m |
| ث | th | ز | z | ع | ‘ | ن | n |
| ج | j | س | s | غ | gh | هـ | h |
| ح | ḥ | ش | sh | ف | f | و | w |
| خ | kh | ص | ṣ | ق | q | ي | y |

With a *shaddah*, both medial and final consonants are doubled.

*Vowels, diphthongs, etc.*

| | | | | | | |
|---|---|---|---|---|---|---|
| Short: | ـَ | a | ـِ | i | ـُ | u |
| Long: | ـَا | ā | ـِي | ī | ـُو | ū |
| Diphthongs: | | | ـَوْ | aw | | |
| | | | ـَيْ | ay | | |

# PREFACE

This brief presentation is written at the request of my very dear friend Shehzad Ahmed. He kept persuading me, for many years, to write something simple and concise on the Shariah to explain its meaning, scope and operation in practical life, which would also help in understanding and appreciating its value and necessity in the believer's life. Such an endeavour is also necessary to dispel the negative and damaging coverage of the Shariah in the Western media. Its adverse portrayal spurs abhorrence in non-Muslims and causes embarrassment to some Muslims who lack proper knowledge.

In Chapter I, I try to address the meaning, components and sources of the Shariah. I also briefly discuss the main objectives of the Shariah as well as the Islamic legal maxims to elucidate the Shariah's humane, compassionate and benevolent attitude when dealing with human affairs. In the following Chapter, the Shariah's guidance for establishing a just and caring society is discussed again, highlighting its enlightened and civilising nature. Issues such as the harsh penal punishments, the treatment of women, homosexuality and apostasy and such like topics, that often raise concerns about the Shariah, are dealt with in Chapter III. In the next chapter the process of the Shariah's implementation in personal life, society and the state are fully discussed. The chapter demonstrates that the whole process of the Shariah's implementation has to be introduced gradually and willingly, and not by force, even in Muslim countries. This also shows that the call to introduce the Shariah instantly is inappropriate and inconsistent with the Islamic approach. In the concluding chapter, I summarise the Shariah's characteristics and its universal and holistic approach. The Bibliography will help those who want to pursue further reading on this topic. For those who just want to know what is lawful and what is prohibited in Islam, I recommend Sheikh Yusuf al-Qaradawi's *The Lawful and the Prohibited in Islam*. This book comprehensively covers most subjects such as food and drink, work and earning a living, clothing and adornment, marriage and family life as well as recreation and play.

This book could not have been completed without the help and guidance of my very dear brother, Prof. Khurshid Ahmad, who, despite his heavy commitments, thoroughly read the manuscript and suggested many changes and improvements. He also arranged for me the procurement of several books on *Maqāṣid al-Shariah* from Pakistan. Again, at his suggestion, I have included a few more topics as well as a section on the explanation of the fundamentals of the Shariah as an Appendix. This is reproduced from a book by Sardar Sher Alam Khan entitled *The Role of the Judiciary and the Objective Resolution* published by the Institute of Policy Studies, Islamabad. I thankfully acknowledge the generosity of the Institute for permission to reprint it. I am most grateful to Prof. Khurshid Ahmed for all his support.

I am also indebted to Prof. Salman Nadvi for reading the manuscript and providing very useful comments and suggestions. I am equally thankful to Prof. Abdur Raheem Kidwai for going through the manuscript and suggesting the inclusion of a few more topics under the section of *Issues of Concern Regarding the* Shariah. The comments of Shehzad Ahmed and Hasan Ahmed were equally useful, which encouraged me to continue the work. Last but not least, I am profusely indebted to Dr. Anis Ahmad for his critical assessment of the manuscript and suggestions.

I would be failing in my duty if I didn't acknowledge the help of the Islamic Foundation Library. I am grateful for the help of Br. Muhammad Sadiq for tracing books and references and Br. Abdul Hayee, the Librarian.

I praise Allah, the Most Gracious and the Most Merciful, Who gave me the *tawfiq* to produce this work. I pray that this short introduction will help readers to understand and appreciate Allah's Mercy in bestowing upon us His blessing by providing guidance through His Shariah.

**Abdur Rashid Siddiqui**
21st August 2017
18 Dhū al-Qiʿdah 1438

## CHAPTER I

# THE SHARIAH: MEANING, SOURCES AND OBJECTIVES

The Shariah is one of the most misunderstood, even maligned, Islamic terms. The word conjures up images of the inhuman, primitive and uncivilised practices of whipping criminals, stoning adulterers, chopping off the hands of thieves and confining women within their homes or only allowing them to venture out enshrouded in a burqa, usually black and covering them from head to toe. No wonder that non-Muslims fail to understand why Muslims yearn for the introduction of the Shariah. To some extent, Muslims are to blame for the creation of this confusion. Whenever they call for the establishment of an Islamic state, their first priority is the introduction of the Islamic penal laws. However, one should not forget that the thirteen years that the Prophet spent in Makkah were dedicated to building an Islamic society and imbibing it with Islam's fundamental tenets of faith. Moreover, during that early period, Allah had not yet sent down all the laws and regulations. But even in Madinah, the laws were prescribed gradually while the penal laws were revealed much later. Thus, the introduction and enforcement of the penal laws right at the beginning is contrary to the religion's strategy for social change and the spirit of the Prophet's way. In such a context, there is a need to explain to both Muslims and non-Muslims what the Shariah is exactly and the process of its implementation.

## The Meaning of the Shariah

Shariah literally means a way or a path and, more specifically, the way to a watering place. In Islamic terminology, after accepting Allah's *dīn* (Religion), the way to be followed, as shown by His guidance and that of His Messenger, is the Shariah. This is the path and source of guidance for humankind and its success in this world and salvation in the Hereafter. This guidance, which is revealed by Allah through His Messenger, covers all aspects of life: beliefs, acts of worship, social transactions and morals. *To each among you have We prescribed a Way* (Shariah) *and a Way of Life* (al-Mā'idah 5: 48); *Then, We put you on the (right) Way* (Shariah)*: so follow you that (Way) and follow not the desires of those who know not* (al-Jāthiyah 45: 18); *He has prescribed for you the Religion which He has enjoined upon Noah and which was revealed to you (O Muhammad), and which We enjoined upon Abraham* *and Moses and Jesus, commanding: 'Establish this dīn and do not split up regarding it'* (al-Shūrā 42: 13).

Thus, the Shariah is a Divinely ordained system to guide mankind straight to the path of righteousness in this world and the acquisition of bliss in the Hereafter. How a person follows the guidance provided in this world will be judged by Allah depending on whether he acted in sincerity and seeking the other world or was he totally immersed in this world. This is the difference between Divine laws and human laws. The latter are only concerned with the interests of this world while the Shariah governs a Muslim's entire life, from birth to death and even beyond.

## The Difference between *Dīn* and the Shariah

The key difference is that the *dīn* (Way of Life) brought by all the earlier messengers before the Prophet Muhammad (peace and blessing be upon him), who was the seal of all prophets and messengers, was, has been and shall always be one and the same. Many Shariahs were revealed; some were subsequently replaced or altered but there was no change in the *dīn*. All the prophets and messengers of Allah (peace be upon them all) presented the same *dīn* but their Shariahs differ to some extent. For example, the prescribed ways of performing the prayer and observing the fast were different under the Shariahs of the earlier prophets. But as the Qur'ān mentions the prayer, *Zakah* (the poor-due) and fasting were an integral part of all earlier Shariahs. Thus, the *dīn* remained the same throughout while the precise details of following it differed from one Shariah to another.

## The Components of the Shariah

The Shariah encompasses a believer's entire life. Its most important aspects are *ʿAqā'id* (the basic tenets of faith) which lay down the relationship between man and God. Essentially, there are three fundamental tenets of faith: *Tawḥīd, Risālah* and *al-Ākhirah*, that is, the belief in the Oneness of Allah, Prophethood and the Hereafter. The entire edifice of Islamic civilisation is based on these fundamental tenets of faith. If *Īmān* (faith) is weak, not only does it weaken other tenets of faith, it also destroys morality, the social structure and the entire culture and civilisation of Muslims. These tenets of faith are briefly explained below:

### *Tawḥīd (Oneness of God)*

*Tawḥīd* is the bedrock of all Islamic tenets of faith. All other tenets of faith are subsumed under *Tawḥīd*. The name Allah (God) is used exclusively for the One Who created the heavens and the earth and everything in this universe. He is not only the Creator but also the only true Provider (*Rabb*). He bestowed upon men and women all their faculties of seeing, hearing and thinking. He provided all the resources for men and women to live in comfort in this world. None is worthy of worship except Allah.

### *Risālah (Prophethood)*

The other tenet of faith is the institution of Prophethood. Just as God has provided for the physical needs of human beings, it is inconceivable that He would not cater for their greatest need: what to believe and how to live in this world. For this purpose, He sent down the prophets to guide mankind. The first Prophet Ādam (peace be upon him) was promised, when he was sent down to earth, that *...guidance shall come to you from Me: then, whoever will follow my guidance need have no fear, nor shall they grieve* (al-Baqarah 2: 38). Throughout human history, prophets came to keep societies on the right path as directed by God but the teachings of earlier prophets were corrupted or forgotten due to the passage of time. Some of these prophets (known as messengers) were also gives Divine scriptures. Muslims are therefore required to believe in earlier holy books such as the Scrolls (*Ṣuḥuf*) of Abraham (Ibrāhīm), the Torah given to Moses (Mūsā), the Psalms of David (Dāwūd) and the Gospel of Jesus (ʿĪsā) (peace be upon them all). The authentic teachings of earlier revelations are referred to in the Qur'ān. For example, the Ten Commandments are incorporated and extended in *Surah al-Isrā'* (17: 23- 39): fourteen specific commandments are mentioned there.

### *Al-Ākhirah (The Hereafter)*

Human beings shall be accountable to Allah with regard to how faithfully they have followed His guidance. On the Day of Resurrection, they will be judged for all their deeds. Belief in the Last Day makes people realise that this world is transitory and finite. On that Day, all creation will be destroyed and people will be raised from their graves. They will stand before their Lord Who will judge their deeds. Thereafter, they will be rewarded or punished according to their good or evil deeds. This sense of accountability before

Allah keeps people on the path of righteousness and makes them steadfast in their *Īmān* (belief) and action.

### *ʿIbādāt (Acts of Worship)*

After accepting some basic tenets of faith, which bring the believing person to the fold of Islam, the other important duties one is required to follow are called the *ʿIbādāt (*sing. *ʿIbādah*, act of worship). These include the performance of the five daily prayers, the obligatory poor-due (*Zakah*), fasting in the month of Ramadan and undertaking the pilgrimage to Makkah (Hajj) once in one's life-time if one can afford it. Thus, the Shariah prescribes detailed rules and regulations for performing these essential duties. Not only do these acts of worship strengthen people's relationship with their Creator, they also create bonds of brotherhood among the believers, as these *ʿibādāt* are communal.

### *Muʿāmalāt (Social Transactions)*

The other area covered by the Shariah is called *Muʿāmalāt* (Social Transactions). These include social life within the family and society at large and laws governing trade, commerce, politics, governance, treaties between nations and laws of war and peace. Essentially, the Shariah comprehensively covers social, economic, political and international affairs. Social transactions cover a wide range of human and non-human life, including the rights of animals, vegetation, etc., even though their major part covers laws governing human relationships.

Allah's sovereignty demands that His rules and commands be applied on the entire universe including mankind.

The natural world follows His laws and commands involuntarily. With mankind, these rules and commands are to be followed by choice. Man's submission to Allah's rules and will and his readiness to live in compliance with His commands is what the Shariah is all about. The penal laws form just a small part of the Shariah. Consequently, one should not give them an unwarranted prominence when discussing the Shariah. Moreover, while following some parts of the Shariah rests with the individual, as is the case with the acts of worship, other parts are the responsibility of the Muslim society, while others require the intervention of the state. Looking at the history of the first Islamic State in Madinah, one notices that the ordinances enforcing the penal laws were revealed towards the end of the Madinan period. Some laws, such as the prohibitions of wine and *ribā* (usury), were revealed gradually. This suggests that society has to be fully prepared for the implementation of these laws (this is discussed fully in Chapter IV below).

## The Sources of the Shariah

Usually, books on Islamic law mention four sources of the Shariah: the Qur'ān, the Sunnah (practice) of the Prophet (peace and blessings be upon him), *ijmā*ʿ (Scholarly Consensus) and *ijtihād* (Independent Juristic Reasoning). However, *ijmā*ʿ takes place as a result of the *ijtihād* of the Companions or, later on, other jurists. So, in fact, there are only three sources of the Shariah. These terms are briefly explained below:

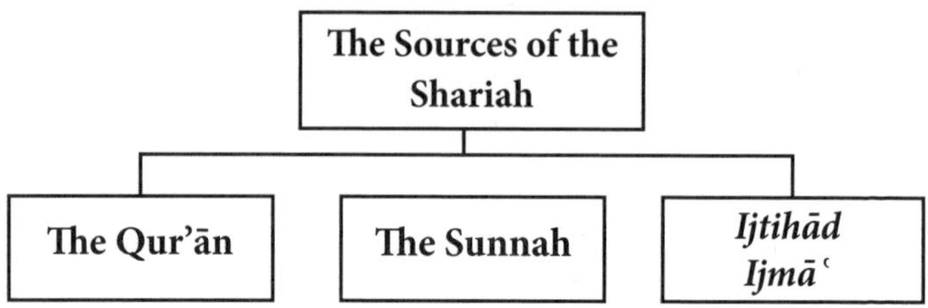


### *The Qur'ān*

The Qur'ān is Allah's speech sent down to the Prophet Muhammad (peace and blessings be upon him) through the Archangel Jibrīl (Gabriel). It is inimitable, unique and protected from corruption by Allah. The Qur'ān is a Book of Guidance. Its purpose is to provide guidance for human beings so that they can fulfil their role of vicegerency and stewardship on earth in order to live a life of moral excellence here and attain salvation in the Hereafter. Thus, the Qur'ān covers a vast number of subjects: moral, social, economic, political and legal, as well as matters relating to creed and metaphysics.

### *The Sunnah*

While the Qur'ān gives basic principles regarding how life on earth is to be lived, the Prophet (peace and blessings be upon him) demonstrated through his practice how these principles were to be implemented. He was the model that the believers are required to follow. During his prophetic ministry, he reformed men, changed society, organised a community and established a state inspired by the guidance provided in the Qur'ān. In this way, the Sunnah is the second source of the

Shariah. The authority of the Sunnah is based on the explicit statements recorded in the Qur'ān to this effect.

The Sunnah is preserved by the *ummah*'s continuous consensus from the time of the Prophet (peace and blessings be upon him) about his practical example. It is also recorded in the books of Hadith, which are collections of the Prophet's sayings, actions and tacit approval.

### *Ijtihād/ Ijmā*ʿ *(Independent Juristic Reasoning)*

This is an Islamic legal term which refers to the use of reason and judgement to determine Shariah rulings. This comes into operation when both the Qur'ān and the Sunnah are silent on a particular issue. This can only be undertaken by thoroughly competent scholars. They can arrive at their opinion (*ra'y*) by using analogy (*qiyās*), juristic preference or equity or public good. *Ijtihād* provides a mechanism to derive guidance with regard to new issues and problems faced by the community.

The consensus or agreement reached on a specific issue through independent juristic reasoning during the time of the first four Rightly-guided Caliphs and the Prophet's Companions is called *Ijmā*ʿ *al-Ṣahābah* (the consensus of the Prophetic Companions). This is accepted as binding. Later scholarly consensus by qualified Muslim jurists may be followed, but it can be changed subsequently by other scholarly consensuses. Today, it is possible that jurists living in a particular country arrive at a consensus on a particular issue. But this consensus will be acceptable elsewhere, or globally, only when an assembly of world renowned jurists and scholars endorse it. *Ijmāʿ* provides a good mechanism for maintaining the unity of the community in the face of changing situations. Thus, *ijtihād* is a vital tool which ensures the Shariah's dynamism and enables the *ummah* (the faith-community of Islam) to face new challenges as and when they arise.

## The Categorisation of Human Actions

As we have seen, the Shariah covers all human activities and provides guidance in the form of a code of behaviour and conduct. The Shariah divides human acts into the following five categories:

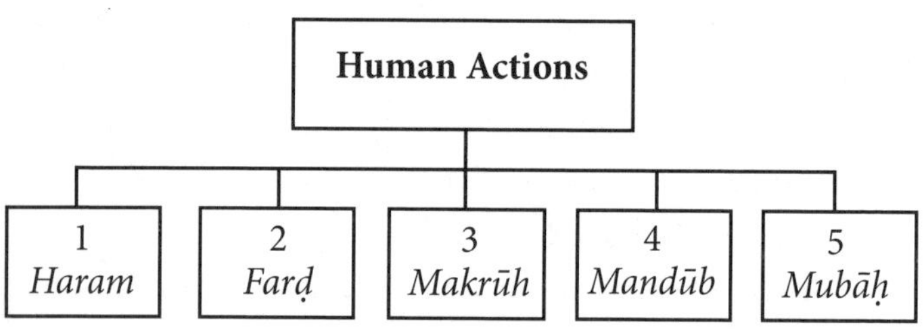


1. Acts expressly prohibited (*haram)*;
2. Acts expressly commanded (*farḍ or wājib*);
3. Acts disliked but not expressly prohibited (*makrūh*);
4. Acts recommended but not enjoined (*mandūb*);
5. Acts about which no specific injunction is given, hence permitted through silence (*mubāḥ*).

This categorisation is a great blessing proffered by the Shariah. Only a few things are prohibited and just a few acts are expressly commanded, which means that a huge degree of latitude and freedom of action is given to individuals and societies. The major part of people's day-to-day life falls into the category of *mubāḥ*. Thus, they have complete freedom of action to decide how to conduct their life.[1]

1 Khurram Murad: *Shari'ah: The Way to God*. Leicester: The Islamic Foundation, 1981, pp. 17–18.

CHAPTER 2

# *MAQĀṢID AL-SHARIAH* (THE MAIN OBJECTIVES OF THE SHARIAH)

## A Brief Introduction

The Islamic legal system developed gradually over the ages and attained maturity in the 5th century AH (10/11 CE). There were a number of theories of interpretation applied by the jurists to interpret the two basic sources of the Shariah. Imam Abū Ḥāmid al-Ghazālī (d. 505 AH/1111CE) propounded that, instead of following the narrow syllogism used by the traditional methods, a wider form of reasoning should be undertaken with reference to the purposes of the Shariah. Many of the details he presented were based on the writings of his teacher, *Imam al-Ḥaramayn* Abū al-Maʿālī al-

Juwaynī (d. 478 AH/1085 CE), especially his book *al-Burhān*. However, the credit goes to Imam al-Ghazālī for organising the theory in a systematic manner. His book *Shifā' al-Ghalīl fī Masālik al-Ta'līl* is entirely devoted to his new theory.[2&3]

A distinctive feature of this book is that al-Ghazālī built his theory from the practices and decisions of earlier jurists, thus demonstrating that he was not inventing something new. Like a legal philosopher, he analysed how the system worked and then formulated a theory to explain how judges discover and apply the law.[4]

## The Contribution of Imam al-Ghazālī

Imam al-Ghazālī divided the purpose of the Shariah into two categories: the *dīnī* (pertaining to the Hereafter) and the *dunyawī* (purposes dealing with this world). He further divided worldly purposes into four types: *ḥifẓ al-nafs* (the preservation of life), *ḥifẓ al-nasl* (the preservation of progeny), *ḥifẓ al-'aql* (the preservation of the intellect) and *ḥifẓ al māl* (the preservation of wealth). When all types of purposes are taken together, one finds that there are five ultimate purposes: the *dīn* (religion), life, progeny, the intellect and wealth.

---

2 Mohammad Hashim Kamali: *Shari'ah Law: An Introduction*. Oxford: Oneworld Publications, 2008, pp. 33-4, and Mahmud Ahmad Ghazi: *Muḥāḍarāt-e-Fiqh*. Lahore: Al-Faiṣal Nāshrān, 2005, pp. 310-317.

3 Imran Ahsan Khan Nyazee: *Theories of Islamic Law: The Methodology of Ijtīhād*. Islamabad: International Islamic University, 1995, pp. 191–193.

4 Op. cit., pp. 193-194.

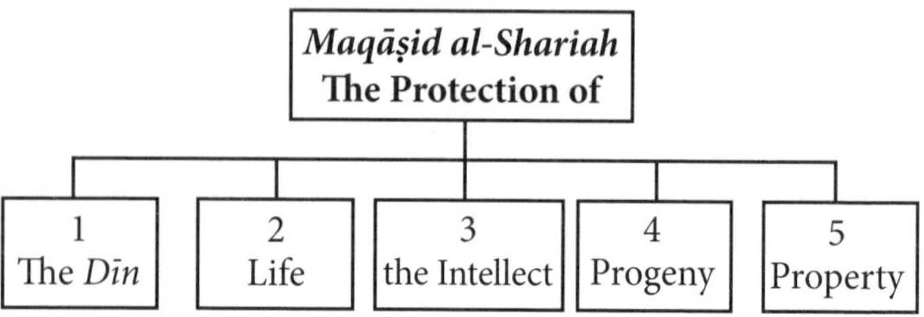


These main objectives are explained below:

- The protection of the *dīn* is the primary objective as it relates to man's relationship with God, which has to be maintained at all cost.
- The protection of life is essential as without human existence there would be no Shariah implementation. Hence, to kill someone unlawfully is like killing the whole of humanity.
- The intellect is the faculty which distinguishes man from other creatures. Thus, its protection is very important. The consumption of intoxicants and drugs that impair this faculty is prohibited. Similarly, practices such as sorcery and witchcraft, which affect its use, are prohibited.
- In order for the human race to continue its existence, it is necessary to protect progeny. For this reason, the family is a Divine institution whose preservation is necessary.
- The security of property, whether it belongs to the individual or the state, is important. Wastage of resources, for example, or their inappropriate use, as well as stealing are considered criminal offences.

Justice in society is the end objective of these five categories. These five purposes are described as *ḍarūriyyāt* (necessities), i.e. they may cause irreparable damage to mankind if not addressed immediately. For example, if a building catches fire, the fire has to be tackled without delay for the sake of the occupants' safety and their property. These are followed by the *ḥājiyyāt* (needs) the lack of which may cause hardship. For example, a lack of adequate heating and hot water in winter is likely to make life very difficult. The third category is the *taḥsīniyyāṭ* (complementary comforts), which may be called embellishments. For instance, a person with lawful resources may spend as much as he likes to achieve the best standard of living suitable for him.[5]

## The Contribution of Imam al-Shāṭibī

Basing himself on the valuable work on *maqāṣid al-Shariah* formulated by al-Ghazālī and his successors, Imam Abū Isḥāq al-Shāṭibī (d. 790 AH/1388 CE), a Spanish scholar who lived in Granada, further refined and advanced the work on the *maqāṣid*. In his most important book, *al-Muwāfaqāt*, he addressed the higher objectives of Islamic law and attempted to perfect their formulation. The five essential purposes are viewed by him as the root or foundation of all other interests. He maintained that the inductive method should be used instead of deriving the *Aḥkām* (legal rulings) from the Qur'ān and the Sunnah by deduction. He also maintained

---

5 Mohammad Hashim Kamali: *Shari'ah Law: An Introduction*. Oxford: Oneworld Publications, 2008, pp. 33-34.

that the *maqāṣid* are definitive (*qaṭʿī*) and can be relied on without fail, as the same pattern can be observed in other details of the Shariah. He quoted many Qur'ānic verses in support of his view. The idea that the *maqāṣid* are definitive, derived through a process of induction from the texts, runs throughout al-Shāṭibī's work.[6]

Understanding the structure of the *maqāṣid* requires the appreciation of their internal relationship and also their connection to other subsidiary and supporting purposes. Al-Shāṭibī provided basic rules along with their detailed explanations. According to him, the first purpose of the Shariah is the safeguard of man's interest pertaining to the Hereafter. The identification of this interest is not left to the whims and fancies of human beings. Establishing what is beneficial or harmful with regards to the Hereafter cannot be left to human reason.

Al-Shāṭibī also identified a dual feature in the *maqāṣid*, for which he uses the terms *ibqā'* (preservation) and *ḥifẓ* (protection). Thus, each purpose has a positive, sustainable and protective aspect. From the positive aspect of each purpose, the provisions or conditions required by the Shariah are secured. Thus, the interest of the *dīn* is secured by providing facilities for worship and other pillars of Islam. Similarly, the interest of life is protected by creating conditions to secure its existence and the existence of progeny by facilitating family life. The interest of the intellect and wealth are secured by promoting the means of their growth. As for

6 Nyazee: *Theories of Islamic Law*, p. 231.

the protective aspect, which is the defensive mechanism, it aims to prevent the destruction or corruption of the positive aspect. Thus, jihad is prescribed for defending the *dīn*. Life is preserved through the prohibition of suicide and unlawful killing. Progeny is secured by the institution of marriage and through imposing penalties on illicit relationships. The intellect is secured through the promotion of education and the prohibition of consuming intoxicants. Wealth is secured by punishing misappropriation, theft and gambling.[7]

## Contemporary Discourses: Extensions and Expansion of the Classical Formulation

Later scholars extended the list of the main objectives of the Shariah and included such things as the dispensation of justice, relieving poverty and the provision of social security. They argued that the main objectives of the Shariah should not concentrate on protection only but should also include the enhancement of the quality of life. Likewise, current national and international problems facing humanity, such as control of the environmental pollution, the protection of natural resources, the prohibition of biological, chemical and nuclear weapons, also require Islamic guidance so that the grave challenges of globalisation can be tackled successfully. In this respect, Dr Mohammad Najatuallah Siddiqui has proposed adding the following main objectives of the Shariah:

---

7 Ahmad Al-Raysuni: *Imam Al-Shāṭibī's Theory of the Higher Objectives and Intents of Law*. London: The International Institute of Islamic Thought, 2006, pp. 108-112.

- Human honour and dignity;
- Basic human rights;
- Justice and equity;
- Alleviation of poverty and provision of social security;
- Social equality and equitable (as defined by the Shariah) distribution of wealth;
- Peace and security;
- Cooperation and participation at the international level as long as it is not against the interests of Islam and Muslims.

This learned author has justified the inclusion of these objectives on the basis of specific Qur'ānic injunctions and Hadiths, which he quotes extensively.[8] Similarly, Sheikh Yusuf al-Qaradawi has extended the list of the *maqāṣid* to include social welfare and support (al-*takāful*), freedom, human dignity and human fraternity. Mohammad Hashim Kamali proposed the inclusion of 'economic development and the strengthening of R&D (research and development) in technology and science to the structure of *maqāṣid*....'[9]

One can clearly see from this list that the Shariah covers the entire range of human activities. Through the mechanism of *ijtihād*, all new issues facing humanity can be addressed by the Shariah. With the advent of the 21st century, rapid changes have been taking place and the Muslim *ummah* is

---

8 Mohammad Najatuallah Siddiqui: *Maqāṣid-e-Sharī'ait*. Islamabad: Idārah Taḥqīqāt-e-Islāmī, 2099, pp. 20-32.

9 Mohammed Hashim Kamali: *Maqāṣid Al-Sharī'ah Made Simple*. London: The International Institute of Islamic Thought, 2008. p. 12

facing many problems. Several *Fiqh* and Shariah councils have been established in many countries to resolve these problems. For example, the European Council for Fatwa and Research, which consists of a number of respectable scholars based in Europe and the Muslim world, provides guidance to Muslim communities living in the West.

## The Islamic Legal Maxims (*al-Qawāʿid al-Fiqhiyyah*)

Like the *Maqāṣid al-Shariah*, the legal maxims convey the spirit, rationale and philosophy of Islamic law. They are in fact axioms and, as such, are universally recognised as true. In law, these maxims are regarded as postulates, i.e. things assumed to be true for the purpose of argument. Thus, the legal maxims are interpretative aids for the jurists where there are no applicable texts in the sources of the Shariah.

The legal maxims are in the form of brief statements, which the jurists have identified through a process of induction and which express the Shariah's principles. These legal axioms are rules of thumb based on the *maqāṣid* and Islamic norms and injunctions. These statements, whose wordings are often taken from the Qur'ān and hadiths, provide guiding principles and general rules which apply to all related particulars. The legal maxims generally express and convey the spirit and philosophy of Islamic law. This is why many Muslim scholars treat them as an extension of the *maqāṣid*.

Based on the *maqāṣid,* the legal maxims are touchstones and criteria for the jurists to follow. They are extremely important and provide the jurists with the understanding of what the Shariah intends and how its goals can be achieved.

For example, the legal maxim: 'The basis of all acts is objective thereof', requires that the validity or otherwise of an act be judged by its motivation and purpose. Similarly, the legal maxim: 'Hardship begets ease' conveys that the spirit of Islamic law is the removal of hardship and the creation of ease.[10]

The most comprehensive and broadly based of all legal maxims are called Universal Maxims (*al-Qawāʿid al-Kulliyah)* and apply to the entire range of *fiqh* without any specification. The jurists have singled out five of these which they consider to be the essence of the Shariah as a whole. These are briefly discussed below:

1. *Acts are to be judged by the intentions behind them*. This is derived from a very well-known hadith narrated by ʿUmar ibn al-Khaṭṭāb who said that he heard the Messenger of Allah (peace and blessings be upon him) saying: 'Actions are but according to intention, and to each man what he intends' (Bukhārī and Muslim). This hadith is of paramount importance. Indeed, some scholars have claimed that it has implications for at least seventy different branches of knowledge. Others have said that this hadith comprises a third of all Islamic knowledge. In the above quoted hadith, the Prophet (peace and blessings be upon him) added by way of explanation: 'Thus he whose migration is for Allah and His Messenger, his migration is for Allah and His Messenger, and he whose migration is to achieve some

[10] Mohammed Hashim Kamali: *Maqāṣid Al-Sharīʿah Made Simple,* pp. 4-5.

worldly benefit or to marry a woman, his migration is for that which he migrated.'

This legal maxim suggests that the intended objective has to be taken into consideration while making any legal judgement. An example given by the jurists is the case of a person who finds some goods on the road, which he takes but they subsequently get lost or destroyed while in his possession. Now his liability depends on his intention. If he intended to find the owner so that he could return the goods to him, then he would be considered a trustee and, as such, he would not have to pay compensation. On the other hand, if his intention was to retain the goods, then he would have to pay compensation to the owner.[11]

2. *Certainty is not overruled by doubt*. This important principle is applied in every area of Islamic Law. It is estimated that the questions that are derived on its basis comprise three-fourths of all legal rulings. This principle is based on the Prophet's statement that one should not assume his *wuḍū'* (ritual ablution) to be invalid on mere suspicion. 'If one of you feels something in his stomach that makes him wonder if anything had passed from him, he should not leave the mosque until he either hears or smells something' (Muslim). Commenting on this hadith, Imam al-Nawawi said that this Prophetic saying sets forth a principle of Islam and a major axiom of Islamic Law, which is that things are legally assumed to

[11] Mohammed Hashim Kamali: *Maqāṣid Al-Sharī'ah Made Simple*, p. 17.

remain as they are unless, and until, it is established with certainty that they are otherwise. Extraneous doubts are of no consequence. (*Sharḥ Ṣaḥīḥ Muslim*)

In ascertaining the degrees of certainty and doubt, Muslim jurists have laid down five categories of proof as follows:

- *Yaqīn* (certainty);
- *Ghalabat al-ẓann* (strong presumption);
- *Ẓann* (presumption);
- *Shakk* (doubt);
- *Wahm* (delusion).

The first three categories are relied upon by the jurists in practical Shariah rulings. For instance, the inheritance of a missing person cannot be executed unless the proof of his death is established, since there is a presumption that he may still be alive. Similarly, all beneficial and harmless things are permissible unless explicitly prohibited by the Sacred Law.[12]

3. *Hardship begets facility*. This means that the presence of difficulty requires that allowances be made to effect ease. Hence, whenever difficulties arise, the law must make provisions to facilitate matters. It is mentioned in the Qur'ān: *Allah intends for you ease and does not intend for you hardship* (al-Baqarah 2:185). In *Surah al-Ḥajj*, Allah says: *He has not laid upon you any hardship*

---

[12] Mohammed Hashim Kamali: *Maqāṣid Al-Sharī'ah Made Simple* , pp. 138-140.

*in religion* (22: 78). This principle is further emphasised by the Prophet (peace and blessings be upon him) who said: 'You have been sent forth to make things easy, not to impose difficulties' (Bukhārī). This is further reinforced by the Prophet's practice as reported by *Umm al-Mu'minīn* 'Ā'ishah who said: 'The Prophet (peace and blessings be upon him) had never been given a choice between two things except that he chose the easiest of the two, as long as no sin was involved in it' (Bukhārī).

4. *Harm must be eliminated.* This means that anything that causes harm must be removed. That which is harmful must be completely avoided whenever possible. When it is not possible to avoid it, then the lesser of two evils should be chosen. Thus, the avoidance of harm takes precedence over the procurement of benefit. This principle is based on the hadith: 'There must be neither harm nor the imposition of harm' (al-Dāraquṭnī and al-Bayhaqī). Thus, if a person's property is destroyed by another person, the person whose property is destroyed is not allowed to destroy the property of the offender in retaliation. If he does so, he will have to pay compensation for the damage he causes.[13] A number of *fiqh* maxims are directly related to, or derived from, this brief hadith. These include the following:

    a. *There is to be neither harm nor reciprocating harm.* An example of the application of this maxim is as

[13] Mohammed Hashim Kamali: *Maqāṣid Al-Sharīʿah Made Simple,* pp. 65-66.

follows: If a tenant's lease on a farmland expires before the harvesting season, he would be allowed to extend it until the harvesting. This is to prevent him from being harmed.

b. *Harm is to be prevented from happening as much as possible.* Examples of this include taking precautionary measures to prevent the outbreak of diseases or to safeguard one's property.
c. *Harm is to be removed or stopped.* Thus, if for instance someone builds a structure which obstructs a public highway, it must be removed.
d. *Harm is not to be removed with a similar harm.* The following example is based on this principle: if one's land is flooded, one should not drain the water into one's neighbour's land.
e. *A greater harm can be removed by a lesser harm.* For example, in time of need, the government can force those who have hoarded goods to sell them at market rate.
f. *Preventing evil takes precedence over bringing about benefit.* An example for this principle would be the selling of tobacco which, although it brings a great deal of economic benefit, should be stopped by the government to prevent its harmful effects on people's health.[14]

---

[14] *Commentary on the Forty Hadith of al-Nawawī* by Jamaal al-Din M. Zarabozo. Boulder: Al-Basheer Company for Publication and Translation, 1999, vol.3, pp. 1154-1157.

g. *A specific harm may be borne to prevent public harm.* If conflict arises between the right of an individual and the right of the public at large, then the jurists acknowledge that it is the right of the state to interfere in the economic activity of people. Hence, it is permissible for the state to levy taxes.[15]

5. *Custom is an acceptable basis of judgement.* This means that customary usage is the determining factor in deciding a case when there is no specific ruling in the Shariah. Custom refers to the prevailing practices of society. However, before following a prevailing custom, certain conditions have to be met. These conditions are:

    a. The custom should not violate any dictates of the Shariah.
    b. The custom is the prevailing practice and is being followed consistently.
    c. The custom must be the clear expression of the usage and there are no other conflicting opinions.
    d. The custom must be of a nature that it has a binding application on the parties concerned.

The basis of this principle is found in the words of the Prophet (peace and blessings be upon him) to the wife of Abū Sufyān, who was a tight fisted man: 'Take for yourself and your children what suffices your

[15] Mansoori: *Shari'ah Maxims*, p. 89.

needs [without his permission] according to what is customary' (Bukhārī).

Ibn Ḥajar al-ʿAsqalānī, in his commentary on this saying, observes: 'He referred her to customary usage in a matter that was not precisely defined in Islamic Law' (*Fatḥ al-Bārī*). Ibn Qayyim also observed that many rulings were given throughout the ages on the basis of custom. Whenever one finds a custom in practice, one must take it into consideration.

It is worth noting that the above five maxims are matters of consensus among all schools of Muslim jurisprudence. Many more maxims were compiled by jurists in order to facilitate the administration of justice and also have modern applications in Islamic finance.[16]

[16] Alan Godlas (comp.): *The Five Universal Maxims of Islamic Law. (al-Qawā'id al-kulliyah al-khams).* http://islam.uga.edu/law_maxims.html and Mohammad Hashim Kamali: *Shari'ah Law: An Introduction.* Oxford: Oneworld Publications. 2008, pp. 144-151.

## CHAPTER 3

# THE SHARIAH'S GUIDANCE FOR ESTABLISHING A JUST AND CARING SOCIETY

### Justice

Justice is the ruling spirit of the Shariah, as Islam wants to establish a just society. The Qur'ān emphasises that the specific purpose for sending down prophets and scriptures is the administration of justice in society: *Indeed We sent Our Messengers with clear signs and sent down with them the Book and the Balance (Right and Wrong) so that people might uphold justice* (al-Ḥadīd 57: 25).

In another place, it is stated that the whole universe has been established on the basis of a harmonious balance. Hence, human beings should not transgress and create imbalance: *And the frmament has raised high, and He has set up the Balance (of justice), in order that you may not transgress (due) balance. So establish the weight with equity, and do not make the balance deficient* (al-Raḥmān 55: 7-9).

Thus, one sees that the establishment of justice and equity in human society is in consonance with what Allah has already established in the universe. The following verse is universally recited by imams throughout the world in their Friday sermon: *Allah commands justice, the doing of good, and liberality to kith and kin, and He forbids all shameful deeds and wickedness and rebellion: He instructs you, that you may receive admonition* (al-Naḥl 16: 90).

This verse from *Surah al-Naḥl* is indeed a very comprehensive set of instructions. Allah's first commandment is to do justice (*ʿadl*). Justice is the fundamental injunction imposed on human beings. The concept of justice, equity and fair dealing is one of the basic tenets of morality which is ingrained in all human beings. So why do people perpetrate injustices on others? What motivates them to transgress the path of fairness and oppress others? Allah, Who knows human weaknesses, identified in the Glorious Qur'ān the reasons for committing injustice as follows: *O you who believe! Stand out firmly for justice, as witnesses to Allah, even against yourselves, or your parents, or your relations, and whether it is (against) the rich or poor: for Allah can protect both. Follow not the lusts (of your hearts); lest you sway, and distort (justice) or decline to do justice, verily Allah is well acquainted with all that you do* (al-Nisā' 4:135).

Injustices manifest themselves because people are swayed more by their self-interests than by their commitment to justice. If decisions affect them personally or their parents or close relations, people are inclined to unjustly defend their position. This is such a serious human failing that Allah has reminded us of it in several places in the Qur'ān: *Believers! Do not be unfaithful to Allah and the Messenger, nor be knowingly unfaithful to your trusts. Know well that your belongings and your children are but a trial, and their lies mighty reward with Allah* (al-Anfāl 8: 27-28); *Your possessions and your offspring are nothing but a trial for you. And there awaits a great reward for you with Allah* (al-Taghābun 64: 15).

The other motive influencing human decision is the status of the concerned parties in a dispute. Often, people tend to favour the rich and those who are influential in society and, thus, stray from the path of justice. Conversely, sometimes, out of pity for the poor people, they decide to favour them. Both attitudes are wrong, as Allah is the best of protectors. If people were truly conscious at all times that Allah is watching them, they would not be unduly swayed by self-interest or favouritism.

Another reason why people are diverted from the path of justice is identified by Allah in this verse: *O you who believe! Stand out firmly for Allah, as witnesses to fair dealing, and let not the hatred of others to you swerve you to wrong and to depart from justice. Be just: that is nearer to piety and fear Allah for Allah is well acquainted with all you do* (al-Mā'idah 5: 8). Enmity towards one's opponents creates feelings of hatred and revenge. Throughout history hatred and revenge have led people to depart from the course of justice and fair dealing, driving them to treat others with contempt and thus undermining their rights. 'My nation right or wrong', has even gained currency among civilised nations. The Islamic teaching is that Muslims should stand firm and be witnesses of truth.

Essentially, the Shariah is based on justice and mercy. Whatever Allah has decreed is to be strictly followed as it is stated: *The word of your Lord is perfect in truthfulness and justice; no one can change His words. He is the All-Hearing, the All-Knowing* (al-An'ām 6:115). Explaining this verse, Khurram Murad writes:

> The Shariah itself is therefore the ultimate criterion of justice and mercy, and cannot and ought not to be measured against changing human standards. Having been given by God, through the last of His prophets, and, therefore, for all time to come, it could not be otherwise....The only absolute and universal criteria can be those given by God, the All-Knowing, whose words are above change.[17]

## Universal Brotherhood

Society in Islam is an association formed according to Divine Law for the purpose of creating a harmonious and peaceful co-existence. It is a scheme of life where the Oneness of God (*Tawḥīd*) is expressed in the Unity of Man. The logical conclusion of this belief is that Islamic society

---

17 Khurram Murad: *Shari'ah: The Way of Justice*. Leicester: The Islamic Foundation, 1981, pp. 12-13.

is neither sectarian nor racial but rather harmonious and universal. According to Islam, differences between human beings on the basis of race, colour, countries of birth or language are natural and can be a basis for nationhood and social existence. It is only beliefs, principles and ideas that distinguish one person from another. On this basis, Islam seeks to build a principled society which is very different from the racial, nationalist societies that exist today. The Islamic social order transcends all geographical boundaries and barriers of race, colour and language. Thus, Islam is suitable for all parts of the world and for all races as its foundation is the universal brotherhood of mankind. The Qur'ān categorically states: *O Mankind! Reverence your Lord, Who created you from a single person, created, of like nature, his mate, from them twain scattered (like seeds) countless men and women; reverence Allah, through Whom you demand your mutual, rights, and (reverence) the wombs (that bore you): for Allah ever watches over you* (al-Nisā' 4: 1); *O Mankind! We have created you from a single (pair) of male and female, and made you into nations and tribes, that you may know each other (not that you may despise each other). Verily the most honoured of you in the sight of Allah is (he who is) the most righteous of you. And Allah has full knowledge and is well-acquainted (with all things)* (al-Ḥujurāt 49: 13).

These verses clearly state that all human beings are one family. Hence, the welfare of each one of them should be a common concern. Sheikh Saʿdī (1196-1226), a renowned Persian poet, composed the following couplets, which are included in his famous *Gulistān,* capturing the message of the above verses:

> *Human beings are members of a whole*
> *In creation of one essence and soul.*
> *If one member is afflicted with pain*
> *Other members uneasy will remain.*
> *If you've no sympathy for human pain*
> *The name of human you cannot retain!*
> (translated by M. Aryanpoor)

There is a clear message here that all men are equal and deserve mutual respect and honour. Similarly, all nations are equally valuable in God's sight. Islam detests any one nation's hegemony over other nations. The Qur'ān makes it amply clear that it rejects the domination of any individual over another individual or any nation over another nation: *As for the Abode of the Hereafter, We shall assign it exclusively for those who do not seek exaltation or corruption in the land; and happy end is for the God-fearing* (al-Qaṣaṣ: 28: 83).

This message of the equality of all human beings, whether Muslim or non-Muslim, is emphatically stated by the Prophet (peace and blessings be upon him) in his farewell address at the last Hajj he performed: 'O people! Surely your Lord is one and your father is one. You all belong to Adam and Adam was created of clay. No Arab is superior to a non-Arab and vice-versa. No white person is superior to a black person and vice-versa. Surely the noblest among you are the most God-fearing.'

Universal brotherhood demands that all problems faced by humanity are tackled by all nations together. Consequently, world poverty, global warming, the provision of basic rights to all, the elimination of weapons of mass destruction, the eradication of terrorism and the exploitation of any nation by another have to be controlled by universal sanctions, help and cooperation. The building of humanity is one of the Shariah's objectives.

## The Sanctity of Life

The sanctity of human life is enshrined in the Shariah as it was in earlier scriptures. *Therefore We ordained the Children of Israel that he who slays a soul unless it be (in punishment) for murder or for spreading mischief on earth shall be as if he had slain the whole mankind; and he who saves a life shall be as if he had given life to all mankind* (al-Mā'idah 5: 32). In this verse, a principle is given to prevent aggression. Thus, if one kills a person, it is as if one has killed all of humanity. On the other hand, saving a life is considered a great deed which equals the saving of all mankind. Islam enjoins the preservation and promotion of life, helps everything that is good to flourish and repels all evil. Its message is one of peace, love and respect for all humanity.

## Moral Values

It is of Allah's mercy that He has given humans basic instincts to differentiate between good and evil. There is an inborn sense of morality in all human beings. Throughout the ages there have been certain qualities that were warmly approved by society, while others were consistently condemned. People appreciate truthfulness, charity, courage, honesty, hospitality, loyalty, sympathy, fidelity, justice and similar good qualities. Likewise, they disdain hypocrisy, bigotry, injustice, falsehood, betrayal, infidelity, cowardice, cruelty and rudeness. When they become part of the collective behaviour of society, these good personal moral values bring about a just, compassionate and morally upright society and state.

It is God who established these moral laws just as He established physical laws to govern the universe. Islam is based on the guidance received from Allah. This guidance ensures that the whole edifice of society is built on good moral values and sets out to generate good and suppress evil. Personal moral values are encouraged and upheld by the wholesome environment of society. In such a society, morality and piety prosper and evil forces are rigorously controlled. The following are some of the basic moral values which Islam wants to inculcate in society.

### *Courtesy and Good Behaviour*

Islam teaches its adherents to treat all human beings with kindness and respect. Even animals and plants have rights in Islam. Of course, one's parents are the first ones to deserve one's utmost reverence: *Serve Allah, and join not any partners with Him. And do good –to parents, kinsfolk and orphans, those who are in need, neighbours who are relations, neighbours who are strangers, the companions by your side, the wayfarer (you meet) and what your right hands possess; for Allah loves not the arrogant, the vain glorious* (al-Nisā' 4: 36).

Kindness to one's parents and relations comes second after the commandment to worship Allah alone. Then, there are the rights of other relations, neighbours, strangers and even wayfarers and servants. For all of them, the Qur'ānic injunction is: *speak kindly to people* (Qur'ān 2: 83). The Prophet (peace and blessings be upon him) said: 'To speak a kind word is charity (for which one deserves a reward from Allah)' (Bukhārī). He is also reported to have said: 'Whoever has no kindness has no virtue' (Muslim).

Neighbours, as mentioned in the above verse, belong to a very wide ambit. They include every person of any faith who has in some way a close relation with one, whether living in the same vicinity, a colleague at work or a companion in a journey on a bus or a plane. The following hadiths illustrate the importance of the rights of neighbours. Abū Shurayḥ al-Khuzā'ī reported that the Prophet (peace and blessings be upon him) said: 'Whoever believes in Allah and the Last Day should be good to his neighbour. And whoever believes in Allah and the Last Day should be generous to his guests. And whoever believes in Allah and the Last Day should say what is good or be silent.' *Umm al-Mu'minīn* 'Ā'ishah related that the Prophet (peace and blessings be upon him) said: 'Jibrīl kept on enjoining me to treat neighbours well until I thought he would make them heirs.' (Both hadiths are from Bukhārī's *al-Adab al-Mufrad*). 'By God he is not a true believer, the one from whose mischief his neighbours are not safe.' (Bukhārī and Muslim).

### *Forgiveness and Pardon*

All humans make mistakes and sometimes even offend others. But one should have the magnanimity to forgive and overlook the shortcomings of others. This is encapsulated in the command of Allah: *Show forgiveness, enjoin what is good and avoid the ignorant* (al-Aʿrāf 7: 199). In *Surah Āl ʿImrān*, Allah praises those, *who restrain their anger, and forgive others. Allah loves such good-doers* (3:134). ʿAbdullāh ibn ʿAmr ibn al-ʿĀṣ reported that the Prophet (peace and blessings be upon him) said: 'Show mercy and you will be shown mercy; forgive and Allah will forgive you' (Bukhārī's *al-Adab al-Mufrad*).

### *The Welfare of Humanity*

The Islamic teachings require that Muslims should work for the welfare of all mankind. It is narrated by ʿAbdullāh ibn ʿUmar that someone came to the Prophet (peace and blessings be upon him) and asked him: 'Who is the best among people?' He replied: 'It is the one who provides the maximum benefit to others.' Numerous sayings of the Prophet indicate that Islam cares for the rights of the weak and the vulnerable, whether they are Muslim or not. Even an enemy deserves kind treatment. The Messenger of Allah (peace and blessings be upon him) said: 'Truly, Allah does not sanctify a nation in which the rights of the weak are not granted' (Baghawī in *Sharḥ al-Sunnah*).

## Economic Justice

Economic exploitation causes much ill-feeling and unrest in society, whereas Islam wants to establish a fair and just social order. Hence, all forms of unjust dealings are declared illegal by the Shariah. These include such things as usurping the possessions of others by deceit, double-dealings or cheating. There are specific injunctions in the Qur'ān which prohibit such acts. *Do not usurp one another's possessions by false means, nor proffer your possessions to the authorities so that you may sinfully and knowingly usurp a portion of another's possessions* (al-Baqarah 2: 188); *Whoever defrauds shall bring with him the fruits of his fraud on the Day of Resurrection, when every human being shall be paid in full what he has earned and shall not be wronged* (Āl ʿImrān 3: 161); *Fill up the measure and do not diminish the goods of people, weigh with an even balance and do not deliver short…* (al-Shuʿarā' 26: 181-183).

Taking interest and interest-bearing transactions are considered forms of exploitation and, hence, strictly prohibited by the Shariah. It is stated in *Surah al-Baqarah: Allah has made buying and selling lawful, and interest unlawful* (2: 275). Islam seeks to establish an ethical economic system with socially responsible investments. It does not put any ceiling on earning/income as long as it is earned in lawful ways and spent in lawful ways. Its economic system is based on the twin concepts of justice and fair play. The current economic crisis has prompted people to reflect on how to transform and reconstruct a better world. In this respect, in the last twenty to thirty years, an Islamic economic system has developed rapidly. In this system, the creation and distribution of wealth is instrumental in promoting individual and social well-being. Many Islamic banks have now been established even in the West with interest-free banking while Islamic bonds may be introduced soon. However, the mere establishment of a few Islamic banks will not bring about any change in the economic system. The capitalist system perpetuates the exploitation of the poor and creates an unjust society. Muslim countries, as a whole, have to take a firm decision to gradually move away from the interest-bearing banking system.

CHAPTER 4

# ISSUES OF CONCERN REGARDING THE SHARIAH

We have tried to present the main objectives of the Shariah and shown how its principles regulate and guide the lives of Muslims and how its teachings are geared to achieving the well-being and welfare of the individual and society. However, there are many misgivings about certain issues for which the Shariah is much maligned. These are briefly discussed in the following pages.

## Women

It is claimed that the Shariah's treatment of women is harsh and unjust. It is correct that women's prevalent condition in many Muslim societies is not a true reflection of the Islamic teachings. This prevalent condition needs to be reformed in line with the high status and significant role assigned to women in Islam. Being biologically and sexually different from men, women's role is different in the family and society. 'Different' does not mean 'deficient' or 'wanting'. The relationship between men and women is complementary. Society's strength depends on the survival of the family and the healthy development of children. The family is the basic unit and building block whose strength consolidates society, while broken families create social problems for the whole society and erode its solidarity. In Islam, men are responsible for providing for their families, while the role of women is childbearing and bringing up the family. This is the most important duty of women. Thus, there is in Islam an equitable division of labour between men and women.

### *The Role of Women*

According to the Shariah, a woman's role is essentially confined to her home. However, this does not mean that her status is in any way inferior to man. There is equality between the sexes regarding spiritual, social, legal and educational participation. But equality does not mean similarity, as men and women perform their duties and responsibilities in their respective domains. Women can fully participate in the social, economic and political life of society. They may work if they feel it is necessary or when they wish to do so. Legally, however, women are not required to spend their incomes on their households or to support their children financially. If they choose to do so, it is only out of their kindness and grace, for it is the duty and responsibility of men to provide for their families. Different Muslim countries have diverse practices regarding the treatment of women. Many restrictions on women, such as not allowing them to pray in the mosque, drive cars or have access to proper education and work, are cultural taboos which are not supported by Islamic teachings. By contrast, there are many Muslim countries with women in positions of leadership. For example, women are in a majority at universities in Iran and the United Arab Emirates. In many countries, such as Turkey, Indonesia, Pakistan and Bangladesh, women hold positions in government and parliament. Nonetheless, many changes in Muslim societies need to be introduced, in accordance with the Islamic teachings, so that women can participate fully in their nations' social, cultural and political life.

### *Polygamy*

Polygamy is another issue which is often highlighted and attacked. It is to be noted that polygamy, as an institution, existed among all nations such as the Hindus, the Jews, the Buddhists and others. It is Islam that reformed this institution by restricting the number of wives to be had to four. Before the advent of Islam, the pagan Arabs used to have an unlimited number of wives. It was fashionable for the chiefs of tribes to have as many wives as they could get. But Islam put an end to this practice. The other stringent requirement for those who opt to have more than one wife is to treat all of them fairly. There should be equality in provision of food, clothing, residence and even sexual relationship. The permissibility of polygamy is granted with the condition that justice is maintained between the co-wives as far as humanly possible, otherwise one has to remain monogamous.

There are several factors which need to be considered regarding the permissibility of marrying more than one wife. Statistically, men and women are almost equal in number in terms of birth rate. However, for a variety of reasons, the number of men in society subsequently decreases. A study of mortality among human beings shows that the mortality rate among men is higher than the mortality rate among women. This disparity is observable in all age groups. As recorded by *Encyclopaedia Britannica*: 'In general, the risk of death at any given age is less for females than for males.'[18] The higher proportion of women in society is also due to a number of other reasons. This was quite noticeable after the two world wars in the last century. In World War I, 8 million soldiers (men) were killed just as most of the civilians killed in this war were also men; whereas the number of casualties in World War II is estimated to be about 60 million. More recently in the Iraq-Iran war (1979-88), nearly 1,800,000 women were widowed in the space of just ten years. There is no shortage of wars and disasters in our troubled world which are behind innumerable deaths and injuries, particularly among men. It is instructive to note that the initial permissibility of polygamy was given after the Battle of Uḥud in 3 A H /625 CE, so that the widows and orphans that this war left behind could be looked after. Thus, it was instigated as a remedial measure for the sake of women

---

18 http://www.britannica.com/science/mortality-demography

and children. It is also worth noting that the Qur'ānic verse which allows marrying more than one wife declares that if one cannot deal equitably and justly towards all wives, then one should marry only one wife.

In some instances, as when one wife suffers from an incurable disease – like paralysis, epilepsy, mental disorder or similar ailments – it is better for one of the other wives to look after the husband and children. The presence of other co-wives may also help the sick one. Similarly, instead of divorcing a wife, after discovering that she is incapable of bearing children, it is better for the husband to keep her as his wife and marry a second wife who may give him children which are one of the joys of family life.

Finally, some men have a very strong sexual desire and cannot be sexually satisfied with one wife. In such cases, polygamy provides the answer, for sex outside marriage is strictly prohibited in Islam and is considered a criminal offence which is severely punished. Instead of having illicit relationships, polygamy provides a better solution for the dignity of women. Islam wants women to be wives, not mistresses.

As Islamic laws are universal and remain valid for all times and cultures, they have to cater for all situations. Yet, despite the permissibility of polygamy, this practice is not widespread among Muslims. Only a minority of Muslims practice polygamy. This view is supported by Ritu Menon, a feminist publisher and independent scholar, who worked on the subject and is the co-author of *Unequal Citizens: A Study of Muslim Women in India*. In her book, she observes that: 'It [polygamy] may be allowed by Muslim personal law, but the incidence rate is not that high.'[19] Other data seems to confirm this. A survey carried out by the Government of India in 1974 puts the polygamy figure at 5.6% among Muslims, and 5.8% among upper-caste Hindus. Research by Mallika B Mistry of the Gokhale Institute of Politics and Economics in Pune in 1993, later recorded by John Dayal, also concluded that 'there is no evidence that the percentage of polygamous marriage (among Muslims) is larger than that among Hindus.'[20]

Although the majority of men would like to have more than one wife, they simply cannot afford it. Even those who are financially capable of looking after additional families are often reluctant to have more than one wife due to the psychological burdens involved in handling more than one wife. Family problems and marital disputes are multiplied in marriages involving more than one wife.

A total ban on polygamy may result in far more serious consequences, as this restriction often leads to illicit extra-marital relations. This can be observed in cultures where monogamy is enforced and where infidelity reaches epidemic proportions. This is the conclusion of Kate Figes in her book, *Our Cheating Hearts: Love and Loyalty, Lust and Lies.* As a writer on relationships and family life for twenty years, she spent three years researching why adultery is now so worryingly common. She writes: 'For the past three years I have examined all of the research, interviewed hundreds of

---

19 Zoya Hasan and Ritu Menon: *Unequal Citizens: A Study of Muslim Women in India*. New Delhi: Oxford University Press, 2006.

20 Mallika B. Mistry and John Dayal: http://scroll.in/article/669083/muslim-women-and-the-surprising-facts-about-polygamy-in-india

experts such as marital therapists, divorce lawyers and people working in "the infidelity business" and talked to 45 men and women who have lived through the experience of an affair themselves. The results were often surprising. Although precise figures remain elusive, surveys in the UK and the US suggest that between 25 and 70 per cent of women — and between 40 and 80 per cent of men — have engaged in at least one extramarital sexual encounter. Therapists told me that approximately three-quarters of men and one-quarter of the women they see individually in their consulting rooms are going through marital difficulties in part because of an affair. Indeed, infidelity appears to be so common in Britain today that it's now more likely than not to occur at some point in a long relationship. Research carried out between 1991 to 2006 on 19,000 people found a rise in the number of both under 35s and over 60s having extramarital liaisons.'[21]

In Islam, the permissibility of polygamy provides a vital safety valve to control this sexual anarchy. Those cultures which outlaw polygamy have to pay a heavy price and must tolerate men and women having illicit relationships and family breakdowns. It is not ideal in Islam to have more than one wife but it is a practical solution to fulfil human needs.[22]

---

21 Kate Figes: *Our Cheating Hearts: Love And Loyalty, Lust And Lies* .London: Virago, 2013. As reported by Daily Mail 13 April 2013. http://www.dailymail.co.uk/news/article-2311947/The-infidelity-epidemic-Never-marriage-vows-strain-Relation

22 Wahiduddin Khan: *Women in Islamic Shari'ah*. New Delhi: The Islamic Centre, 1995, pp. 113-124 and Abdur Rahman I. Doi: *Women in Shari'ah*. London: TaHa Publishers, 1989, pp. 50-67.

### *Hijab*

Hijab is another controversial issue as it is considered a form of victimisation of women and a tool of oppression used by men and governments. Much of the debate on this issue is rather emotional. The fact is that countless Muslim women around the world have chosen to cover their heads and bodies on their own volition rather than being forced to do so. Hijab is worn by these women as a symbol of modesty, privacy and morality. Many women view hijab as a tool of empowerment that allows them to focus on family, work and faith rather than material concerns.

Essentially, modesty and the feeling of shame are imbedded in human nature. In Islamic terminology this is called *Ḥayā'* and is considered part of faith (*īmān*). It is a universal practice to cover one's private parts. Modesty in dress has been an integral part of human nature since the advent of the first human beings. This can be seen from the Prophet Ādam (peace be upon him) and his wife's story when they became aware of their nakedness. Their first instinct was to cover up. As sexual desire is one of the most vulnerable aspects of human nature, Satan tends to exploit it. For this reason, many safeguards are prescribed by Islam so that sexual temptations remain under control. The foremost among these is safeguarding one's gaze. Allah has made fornication, adultery and homosexuality unlawful. In order to protect one's chastity, the Shariah has also blocked all those routes through which people may slip into wrongdoing. The most important injunction in this context is the lowering of one's gaze. Allah instructs in the Holy Qur'ān: *Say to the believing men that they should lower their gaze and guard their modesty: that will make for greater purity for them and Allah is well acquainted with all that they do. And say to the believing women that they should lower their gaze and guard their modesty that they should not display their beauty and ornaments except what (must ordinarily) appear thereof; that they should draw their veils over their bosoms…* (al-Nūr 24: 30-31).

This is such an important command that these verses of *Surah al-Nūr* address both men and women in a similar manner but separately. Thus, these restrictions are imposed on both sexes. Looking at another person, whether male or female, with lust is unlawful. Thus, the Shariah prescribes a specific dress code for both men and women. Men are mandatorily required to cover the area between the navel and the knees, and their clothes should be loose and thick enough so as not to reveal what is covered. And these should not be designed in a way to attract attention. For women, the dress must cover the whole body except the areas exempted by the verse quoted above while their clothes' looseness and thickness have the same requirements as those for men.

To reinforce this injunction for lowering the gaze, the Qur'ān states: *(Allah) knows the treachery of the eyes and all that the hearts conceal* (Ghāfir 40: 19). In order to preserve chastity in society, appropriate dress codes for both sexes have been prescribed as noted above. Restrictions on the social mixing of the sexes also lead to the stability of married life. This fact is well documented and acknowledged in *Encyclopaedia Britannica*. Commenting on the increasing rate of divorce in Western society, it says: 'Actors, authors and other groups that have contacts with the opposite sex tend to have a high divorce frequency.'[23]

The other important teaching of the Shariah on the protection of chastity and family life is the control imposed on sexual conduct by both sexes. Islam absolutely prohibits all forms of sexual deviation and extra-marital sex. It also regulates social behaviour in a manner that minimises the possibilities of sexual misbehaviour. In this respect, it regulates, and discourages, opportunities that may tempt people to moral laxity or sexual proximity. Islam prohibits mixed gatherings, the use of alcohol and establishing illicit relationships.

By prescribing a modest dress code for women, Islam frees them from exploitation and being viewed as sex objects. By dressing in a way that hides their beauty from the preying eyes of men, Muslim women are able to give a clear indication that they should be treated with respect. As Murad Hoffmann, a former German diplomat and scholar, has succinctly and frankly observed:

> Sexuality is not displayed on the streets in the Islamic world. Pornography is not tolerated in public. Girls wanting to get married normally refuse to enter into pre-marital relationships. Illegitimate children are a rarity. Most brides are virgins when they marry. Advertisements for wife-swapping, nudist beaches,

---

[23] http://www.britannica.com/search?query=Rate+of+divorce+in+western+society. *Encyclopaedia Britannica* ,1984, vol.7, p. 163.

> homosexual 'marriages', student communes – none of these exist in Muslim countries. This is how old-fashioned Islam is – and it is proud of it. Men's and women's dress, including the veil, plays an important part in this; for from the Islamic point of view it is logical not to provoke anything undesirable.[24]

## Punishments

The punishments prescribed by the Shariah have been a target of bitter criticism and are projected to be controversial and inhumane. The basic principle on which Islamic punitive laws are prescribed is based on the *Maqāṣid al-Shariah*, as discussed above, and include the protection of religion (*dīn*), the protection of life (*nafs*), the protection of the intellect (*ʿaql*), the protection of lineage (*nasl*) and the protection of property (*māl*). The purpose of these severe punishments is to keep society safe so that people can live in peace and tranquillity. To live in constant fear of being attacked or robbed is certainly an unacceptable state of affairs. The ultimate aim for Muslim society is peace and harmony. If there are no crimes committed, there is no need to impose severe punishments.

One has also to appreciate that punishment is an integral component of any legal system. Even a common person would agree that criminals should be punished. So, let us consider the basic Islamic principles concerning

---

24 Murad Hofmann: *Islam the Alternative*. Reading: Garnet Publishing, 1993, p. 149.

punishments. It is broadly accepted that man has freedom to act, and this freedom comes with responsibility. But as he is responsible for his actions, he has to bear their consequences. If he transgresses against the law and his guilt is proved within the due process of law, then he should be punished. The jurists agree that the punishment must fit the crime. The more severe the crime, the more stringent is the punishment. Through the punishment of an individual who commits a crime, society is saved from crime.

In this context, it is also worth considering Islam's approach to crime prevention and punishment. Islam's basic approach is geared towards crime prevention rather than punishment. The basic Islamic tenets of faith and the obligatory acts of worship create certain character traits in Muslims which help to curb crime in society. These character traits are as follows:

- God-Consciousness (*Taqwā*) and Self-purification (*Tazkiyah*): Islam instils in the hearts of Muslims the certainty of Allah's presence at all times. This consciousness requires them to differentiate between good and evil and disposes them to embrace what is good and shun what is evil. One of the main functions of the Prophet (peace and blessings be upon him) was to inculcate in Muslims both spiritual and physical purification to develop well-rounded human beings. By virtue of these qualities, Muslims are trained to control their minds and their baser instincts and, as a result, indirectly abstain from committing crimes.

It is for this reason that Islam prescribed all the acts of worship – the Prayer, Fasting, *Zakah* and *Hajj* – which constantly remind Muslims that their Creator is watching over their deeds and He knows even that which is hidden in their hearts.

- Accountability on the Day of Judgment: Belief in life after death and accountability for one's actions in this world on the Day of Judgement is part of the basic teachings of Islam. Thus, one remains cautious in one's life and always remembers that one is accountable to Allah for one's deeds and actions in the Hereafter. One may manipulate laws and escape punishment in this world, but there will be no escape or manipulation in the Hereafter. This creates a sense of responsibility and encourages one to lead a life of piety and righteousness.

    Without this belief, life on this earth does not make much sense. One sees many injustices and wrongs being done all around. The perpetrators of such crimes are not always caught nor are they sufficiently punished to fit the crimes they commit. Then there are many pious people who selflessly devote their lives to doing good deeds. They are not always rewarded for their good deeds. This does not seem fair. Hence, if one does not believe in life after death, where people will be punished and rewarded properly for their deeds, all other beliefs become meaningless. Thus, belief in the Day of Judgement has a radical effect on people's lives.

- In Islam every institution is value-oriented and has responsibility vis-à-vis the moral development of every person. Thus, the family, the neighbourhood and society all exert a moral pressure to keep a person within the limits of law. It is particularly the family which teaches good habits and morality to children. Hence, stable relationships between spouses and children help to create law-abiding families that are less likely to engage in criminal activities. Research has shown that it is usually the children of single parent homes or from dysfunctional families who are involved in crimes.[25]
- The institution of *Zakah* and *Ṣadaqāt* (compulsory and voluntary alms) ensure that the poor, the needy and the destitute are properly looked after. In an Islamic system, everyone is entitled to social security. If a person's circumstances are such that he is unable to earn a living due to ill-health, unemployment or disability, then it is the duty of the state to provide food, clothing and shelter for him and his family. This helps to prevent poverty which is likely to lead to crime.

---

[25] Howell, Nicole: A Link Between Single Parent Families and Crime. Ed.D. Dissertations Paper 79. School of Graduate and Continuing Studies, Olivet Nazarene University. 2015. http://digitalcommons.olivet.edu/cgi/viewcontent.cgi?article=1078&context=edd_diss Hymowitz,Kay: The Real, Complex Connection Between Single-Parent Families and Crime. *The Atlantic*, December 3, 2012. https://www.theatlantic.com/sexes/archive/2012/12/the-real-complex-connection-between-single-parent-families-and-crime/265860/

- Islamic law ensures that the opportunities of committing crimes and inducement to crime remain minimal. For this reason, among others provisions, the consumption of intoxicants and intense free-mixing of unrelated men and women are prohibited. From the standpoint of the Shariah, it seems unjust to allow the consumption of alcohol and then punish a person for driving while under the influence of alcohol, or to provide all kinds of temptations and opportunities for unlawful acts and then persecute those who fall for them.

With the above measures, the Shariah protects society from commission of crimes in the first place. Those who ignore this pre-crime reform and go on to commit crimes face robust and appropriate punishments.

### *Categories of Punishments*

There are basically three categories of punishments in the Shariah. The first is *Ḥadd* (pl. *Ḥudūd*) which is a Divinely prescribed punishment based on the Qur'ān and the Sunnah and carried out by the state. The word *ḥadd* means a barrier which prevents two objects from meeting each other. In this case, it prevents people from committing crimes. Here, the purpose of punishment is to discipline the offender and stop him from committing the same act again while deterring others from committing similar crimes. These punishments are set to preserve the public interest; they are fixed and cannot be altered.

*Hudūd Allāh* are the limits set by Allah which must not be transgressed (al-Baqarah 2: 229). The Qur'ān has provided severe punishments to protect four central interests and values of society: public order, private property, sexual order and personal honour. Those who violate these interests – such as bandits, thieves, rapists, paedophiles and slanderers – face severe punishments. The important function of these severe punishments is to deter others and prevent further crimes from happening. The Qur'ān alludes to this aspect by saying that it is: *an exemplary punishment from Allah* (al-Mā'idah 5: 38). These punishments are harsh but the procedures needed before their execution are very strict. Unless guilt is absolutely proven beyond any doubt, the punishment cannot be applied. It is narrated from the Prophet (peace and blessings be upon him) that it is preferable to let nine criminals go free than to convict one innocent person. In another hadith, the Prophet (peace and blessings be upon him) said: 'Prevent the application of *ḥadd* punishment as much as you can and whenever any doubt persists.'

The second category of punishments is called *Qiṣāṣ* (retaliation or retribution), which is the punishment for homicide and assault. When a person causes physical harm to another person, the injured person has the right to inflict a similar injury on the aggressor. This is based on the Biblical injunction of: *an eye for an eye, a tooth for a tooth* (Exodus 21:24). Now this principle is nowadays considered to be primitive and uncivilised. In the Islamic view of history, not everything primitive is necessarily uncivilized. Universal laws are permanent and should not be deviated from merely on the basis of people's whims. Unlike other crimes which are punished by the state, *qiṣāṣ* under Islamic law is dependent on the volition of the injured person. He may choose to forgive the offender or may agree to accept a monetary compensation. The Qur'ān, in fact, highly recommends the act of forgiving those who wrong one. It is not generally recognised that the principle of *qiṣāṣ* may allow the avoidance of even capital punishment. Thus, the Qur'ān mentions: *Hence, there is life for all of you in retribution, O people of discretion and understanding, so that you may be ever God-fearing* (al-Baqarah 2:179). This concept of forgiveness is part of the Islamic system of justice. The ideal way is not to seek revenge at all but to forgive and reconcile in order to make the offender realise the gravity of his crime. This then leads to *tawbah* (repentance) whereby the offender seeks forgiveness by returning to God. The Islamic teachings encourage those who commit sins or transgress against others to seek forgiveness from Allah. Genuine repentance means that one is truly remorseful, ashamed and intent on not repeating the crime committed.

All other crimes fall into the third and last category, *Taʿzīr*, which is a discretionary punishment legislated by the state and enforced by the court. This category includes the most flexible type of punishments as changing social situations are taken into account. They are flexible enough to effectively reform the criminal and reduce the harm inflicted on society. This type of punishment may range from issuing a warning, imposing fines or suspended sentences to imprisonment, depending on the gravity of the crime committed.

The purpose of *Taʿzīr* is to prevent the person from re-offending and also acts as a deterrent for others. A number of factors are taken into consideration when choosing the appropriate *Taʿzīr* punishment, including whether the crime considered is a first offence or not and also whether there are any mitigating circumstances. It also includes punishments enacted by the state or the local authorities for contraventions of such laws and bye-laws as speed limits and parking restrictions.

One obvious purpose of punishing an offender, as we have seen above, is retribution as well as the reform of the offender by encouraging him to seek repentance from Allah. The other purpose is to deter potential wrongdoers from committing similar crimes. Thus, the aim of imposing punishments is the reform of society and the establishment of law and order. Both these purposes are mentioned in the Qur'ān. In the light of this, when all spiritual and mundane needs of a person are adequately provided for, committing crimes in such a context requires harsh punishments. It is also noteworthy that there are in place strict procedures before a person is convicted or punished. Again, in cases of exceptional situations, like famine and drought, some punishments are suspended. This was actually done during the reign of ʿUmar ibn al-Khaṭṭāb, the second Caliph, when there was a famine in Madinah.

Finally, Islamic criminal law can only be fully implemented in a truly Islamic society where Muslims are inclined to steer away from criminal activities because of their God-consciousness and fear of Allah's chastisement in the Hereafter. This prevents them from committing crimes in the first place. There are also other factors which keep Muslims away from crime such as strong family ties and the rejection of criminals by the whole society. The Islamic social and economic order ensures that people's needs are fully provided for and no-one is forced to commit crime in order to meet their basic needs for survival. Islam tries to remove any factors that may lead one to committing crimes. But even if a person goes on to commit a crime after that, Islamic law requires strict proofs of his guilt. And if there is any doubt, then there is no punishment. For example, to convict someone of adultery, four witnesses are required as evidential proof, which is simply impossible in normal circumstances. Hence, in the light of the above discussion, one cannot condemn Islamic penal laws as being too harsh and inhumane. Actually, all forms of punishments regulated by the Shariah are geared towards reforming the offenders and preventing the recurrence of crimes.

### Apostasy

The other concern raised about the Shariah relates to the issue of apostasy. In Islam, *there is no compulsion in religion* (al-Baqarah 2: 256) and one is free to choose what to believe, *so whoever wills – let him believe! And whoever wills – let him disbelieve!* (al-Kahf 18: 29). No punishment is imposed on the unbelievers because of their unbelief, for they are free to accept Islam or reject it. However, once a person makes a choice to become a Muslim, then one is not allowed to repudiate the Islamic faith. Usually people find it difficult to understand the rationale behind this fact or the severe punishment imposed for apostasy. The basic fact which people ignore is the difference between Islam as a religion and Islam as a complete system of life which covers all aspects including the state. There are different sets of rules for these two entities. Islam as religion is a personal choice which is reflected in the acceptance of the Islamic creed and the fulfilment of the religious obligations. In an Islamic state, however, the religion becomes one's ethnicity, culture and social identity – one's religion becomes one's citizenship. In such a scenario, renouncing the Islamic faith becomes an act of treason. This was also the case in other cultures. For example:

- The Holy Roman Empire had its officially sanctioned and legally enforced version of Christianity.
- The Sasanian Empire had its officially sanctioned and legally enforced version of Zoroastrianism.
- In China, Buddhist rulers fought Taoist rulers for political ascendancy.[26]

In early Islamic history, apostasy was used by many mischievous and disgruntled people to sabotage the new faith's rising popularity. They pretended to accept Islam for a short period and then rejected it (Āl 'Imrān 3: 72). Some made a mockery of the faith, as described in *Surah al-Nisā'*:

---

26 Aslan, Reza: *No god but God: The Origins, Evolution, and Future of Islam*. London: Random House, 2011, p. 81.

*Those who believe then reject faith. Then believe (again) and (again) reject faith and go on increasing in unbelief – Allah will not forgive them or guide them on the way* (4: 137). It was therefore decreed that once one chooses to become Muslim and declares loyalty to the Islamic state, one forfeits the option to change one's beliefs and has to abide by the Islamic rules. Thus, after the death of the Prophet (peace and blessings be upon him), some people wished to remain Muslim but did not want to pay the *zakah*; this was not acceptable. The refusal to honour their financial obligations to the Islamic state was treated as an act of treason and those responsible were punished. In all political systems, acts of treason are capital offences.

The other aspect of this issue is that, in Islam, acceptance of faith is a binding contract. This is emphasised in many places in the Qur'ān such as in, *Surely Allah has purchased of the believers their lives and their belongings and in return has promised that they shall have Paradise* (al-Tawbah 9: 111); *O you who believe! Shall I lead you to a bargain that will save you from a grievous penalty? That you believe in Allah and His Messenger and that you strive (your utmost) in the Cause of Allah, with your property and your persons: that will be best for you, if you but knew!* (al-Ṣaff 61: 10–11).

Thus, the acceptance of Islam is a contract between man and God as well as between man, society and the Islamic state. The acceptance of Islam by a person proffers on one many rights but also imposes certain responsibilities on one. Like any other contract, it is usually fairly easy to effect but very difficult to rescind. One cannot just cancel it unilaterally. As stated above, this is considered an act of treason and, hence, its punishment is only applied by the state. Moreover, this is applicable only in a fully-fledged Islamic state, not in any present-day Muslim country even if it declares itself as an Islamic Republic or Kingdom. Present day 'Islamic' republics and kingdoms do not provide Islamic education nor cultivate an Islamic culture that would make their citizens uninclined towards abandoning their Islamic faith. Due to their negligence, many misguided and disgruntled individuals, raised in Muslim families, may choose to disregard their faith, and they are in no position to apply the punishment for apostasy.

The other misunderstanding about the punishment of apostasy is that the person accused of apostasy faces capital punishment in all circumstances. However, there are grades of disbelief – a person may just not believe in some articles of faith or converts to another faith or be actively involved in anti-Islamic activities – so how can anyone think that Islamic law will treat all these different scenarios in the same manner?[27]

Finally, all legal systems have provisions for freedom of action but they also have certain restrictions to this freedom. For instance, one is not free to sell himself to slavery or to commit suicide. Even desertion from the armed forces is considered a crime. This is because a state can use force and coercion as its inherent right to preserve its sovereignty.

---

27 Mawdūdī, Syed Abul 'Alā: *Islāmī Riyāsat*. Lahore: Islamic Publications Ltd., 1962, pp. 488-489.

Thus, apostasy is considered a crime against the Islamic state and this is why it is dealt with harshly.

**Homosexuality**

Homosexuality now enjoys greater acceptance in the West as an alternative lifestyle and it affects adults as well as children who are lured into experimenting with it. Under intense pressure from the Gay Lobby, Section 28 of the Local Government Act 1988, which prohibited the promotion of homosexuality in schools and presenting it as an alternative family relationship, was repealed in 2000. Under the rubric of sex education, children in our schools are taught to respect and tolerate homosexuality. There is no discussion about moral guidance or the sinfulness of homosexuality, as taught by all religions. Earlier, the Sexual Offences Act 1967 stipulated that a homosexual act in private shall not be deemed an offence provided the parties involved consent to it and are 21 years of age. Again, under persistent lobbying from the Gay Rights Movement, the age of consent was reduced to 16. Since the 1970s, a number of demonstrations have taken place in the United Kingdom in favour of abolishing the age of consent, in support of children's rights.

Unfortunately, some religions, besides Islam, are giving way under the pressure of the gay lobby. The opposition of some clerics is muted while others grant their tacit approval to this activity. It is therefore not surprising that Islam is being demonised as a homophobic, fanatical and intolerant religion which persecutes homosexuals. But it is not just

Islam that has outlawed homosexuality. Leviticus Chapter 20 also legislates against homosexuality: *If a man has sexual relations with another man, they have done a disgusting thing and both shall be put to death* (Leviticus: 20: 13).

In the New Testament, there are three references to homosexuality, all of which are in the Pauline Epistles. In two cases, a passing reference is made to homosexuality as a sin within a list of other sins (1 Corinthians 6, 9-10 and 1 Timothy 19-10). It is, however, in the Epistle to the Romans that the main reference occurs: *Because they do this, God has given them over to shameful passions. Even the women pervert the natural use of their sex by unnatural acts. In the same way, the men gave up natural sexual relations with women and burn their passion for each other. Men do shameful things with each other; as a result, they bring upon themselves the punishment they deserve for their wrongdoing* (Romans 1: 26-27).

Homosexuality, like other matters pertaining to sexuality, is also discussed in the Holy Qur'ān and hadiths. The story of the Prophet Lūṭ (Peace be upon him) is narrated in the Qur'ān in several places, warning about the punishment for homosexuality inflicted on his people. He admonished his people saying: '*Do you realise that you practise an indecency which no other people in the world were guilty of before you? You approach men lustfully in place of women. You are a people who exceed all bounds.' Their only answer was: 'Banish them from your town. They are a people who pretend to be pure.' Then We delivered Lut and his household save his wife who stayed behind, and we let loose a shower (of stones) upon them. Observe, then, the end of the evil-doers* (al-Aʿrāf 7: 80-

84). In another *Surah*, the description of their punishment is narrated in more graphic terms: *And when Our Command came to pass, We turned the town upside down, and rained on it stones of baked clay, one on another marked from your Lord* (Hūd 11: 82-83).

The people of Lūṭ were utterly destroyed because they did not listen to the exhortation of their Prophet. If people were really born to commit homosexual acts, Allah who is most Merciful would not have destroyed Prophet Lūṭ's community. These people were warned and had an opportunity to change and reform but they did not and were, consequently, destroyed.

According to some commentators, the following verse in *Surah al-Nisā'* also deals with this issue: *If two persons among you are guilty of lewdness, punish them both. If they repent and amend, leave them alone; for Allah is Oft-Returning, Most Merciful* (al-Nisā' 4: 16).

These teachings, found in all religions, indicate that homosexuality is indeed a violation of human nature and is, therefore, sinful. To counteract this unambiguous religious indictment, there is a strong homosexual lobby which tries to persuade public opinion that people are born gay. The question of how homosexual orientation originates is promoted largely as a matter of genes rather than being due to an environmental factor. However, a closer examination of the scientific literature does not support this claim. There is certainly no 'gay gene'. Eight major studies of identical twins in the United States, Australia and Scandinavia during the last two decades indicate that homosexuals are not born that way. Science has yet to find that genetics is the cause of homosexuality.[28]

Additionally, a distinction is made between having homosexual desires and choosing to engage in homosexual acts. Having an inclination towards homosexuality cannot be condemned as it is not under one's control, but acting upon it is condemnable. Whatever thoughts prevail in one's mind, if one does not act on them and tries to deal with them with a firm conviction that they are sinful, then one can avoid them. One may need the support of caring persons to help one overcome such desires. The best advice is to get married to overcome sexual urges and to regulate sinful desires. Fasting is also recommended to suppress lustful desires.

For those who are involved in homosexual activity, one should deal with them with kindness. Islam encourages its adherents to hate sins and crime, not the people who commit them. There is no question of bullying, ridiculing or oppressing homosexuals, as unfortunately sometimes happens. It is sometimes argued that homosexuality is a natural phenomenon and should not be made illegal. However, not every natural thing is normal. Like any abnormality or aberration, it should be treated. Hence, there may be people who have homosexual tendencies. These people have to control their desires to abide by social and moral codes of behaviour; just as there are other people who have other weaknesses and desires which they have to control. But a sin is a sin and a moral

---

28 http://www.godandscience.org/evolution/genetics_of_homosexuality.html

offence is a moral offence and people must be persuaded to avoid and refrain from them.

As for the punishment for this sin, there is a difference of opinion among Muslim scholars, as there is no specific, prescribed punishment for it in the Shariah. Indeed, Muslim jurists have held differing opinions about the punishment for homosexuality. Such punishment can only be meted out by an Islamic state. For Muslims living in the West, although the issue of homosexuality is controversial and sensitive, it should be discussed dispassionately while, at the same time, resisting the attempt of the Gay Lobby to impose it on society.

## Blasphemy

In all civilised societies, a person's honour and dignity are protected by defamation and slander laws. When one's character is attacked, one can redress the matter through law courts. Strangely, this only applies to living persons, those who have departed from this world are not protected in any way. The Qur'ān proclaims: *Indeed We have honoured the progeny of Adam* (al-Isrā' 17: 70). While delivering a sermon during his final Hajj, The Prophet (peace and blessings be upon him) said: 'Surely your lives, your properties and your honours are as inviolable for you as the inviolability of this [sacred] day, this month and this place' (Muslim). The Qur'ān even asked its followers not to abuse the idols which were worshiped by the polytheists (al-An'ām 6: 108).

The law of blasphemy is designed to protect the honour and dignity of all prophets, who are undoubtedly respected by their followers as well as to combat intolerance, negative stereotyping and the stigmatisation of people on the basis of their religion or beliefs. Anti-blasphemy laws exist in some form or another in the legal code of many countries. The majority of these countries are Muslim. There are also numerous European countries that condemn and penalise blasphemy, 'religious insult' or the 'vilification' of religious feelings and dogmas. Yet, this is only applicable to the Christian faith while Islam and its Prophet are regularly vilified with impunity.

Muslims honour and respect all prophets and value their honours more than they value their own. They feel degraded and aggrieved when the prophets, particularly the Prophet Muhammad (peace and blessings be upon him), are ridiculed and caricatured. This is why the Shariah has a strict law of blasphemy. However, the punishments for blasphemy can only be applied in an Islamic state. In the West, some unscrupulous people, either to incite the sensitivities of Muslims or to gain publicity, resort to defaming such venerable personalities. In order to uphold the dignity and honour of all the prophets, the Organisation of Islamic Cooperation (OIC), on behalf of the United Nations' large Muslim bloc, started a campaign calling for the imposition of worldwide criminal penalties for the 'defamation of religions'. But this was not successful due to lack of support from other countries.

In the wake of protests and violence in connection with the *Innocence of Muslims* (an anti-Islamic video uploaded on YouTube on July 2012), a number of political and religious authorities made fresh calls for the institution of an international law against the 'defamation of religion', or 'blasphemy'.

It was argued that in view of this provocation, there should be international legal regulations against attacks on what people consider sacred. These demands for an international prohibition of 'blasphemy' are not reactionary at all, but they are viewed as a violation of fundamental human rights.

Despite opposition from some Western states, the OIC resolution against the 'defamation of religion' was passed at the then UN Commission for Human Rights and later by the UN Human Rights Council every year. It even got through the UN General Assembly every year up until now. Unfortunately, none of these resolutions were binding and, hence, did not enter international law. Nonetheless, the goal of OIC was to achieve a global mandate for blasphemy law. Unless such an international law is enacted to uphold the dignity and honour of all the prophets and included in the Universal Declaration of Human Rights, all prophets and religions will face constant degradation and ridicule.[29]

## Jihad

Jihad is one of the most misunderstood Islamic terminologies, which is commonly translated as 'holy war'. However, jihad literally means to struggle to one's utmost or to exert one's utmost endeavour in promoting a right cause. Jihad is the Qur'ānic terminology for struggle and means investing one's capabilities and resources through utmost striving –

---

[29] https://en.wikipedia.org/wiki/Defamation_of_religion_and_the_United_Nations

including fighting if need be – so as to obey Allah's commands, seek His good pleasure and establish His *dīn*. Jihad is an all-encompassing term which covers all types of struggle including fighting.

The word jihad is often used as a synonym for war which is not correct. When fighting is specifically meant, other Arabic words like *Ḥarb* (war) and *Qitāl* (fighting) are deliberately used in the Qur'ān. The reason for this is because jihad does not only involve war but has also several other dimensions. These are briefly explained below:

- In one's daily life, one faces a constant struggle to follow the path of righteousness just as one tries to make one's own desires, aspirations, passions, likes and dislikes conform to the Shariah. This is the most important jihad, which is called *Jihād al-Nafs* (struggle against one's own ego). The Prophet (peace and blessings be upon him) said: 'Practise jihad against your carnal self.'
- Those who want to traverse the path of piety face many promptings and whisperings from Satan, who uses insidious ways from within to try to sap one's will. These evil inclinations within one often attempt to make one deviate from the path of righteousness. Jihad against these evil inclinations is jihad against Satan.
- In addition to conquering one's own desires and trying to safeguard oneself against evil thoughts and deeds, one sometimes faces opposition from one's

own family and friends. The piety and religiosity which are reflected in one's life sometimes cause friction as one is seen to be following a different path. Thus, one sometimes faces struggle (jihad) with one's own family, friends and society.

- If one is convinced that one is following the right path, then it is incumbent upon one to call others to this path. This *daʿwah* (invitation), which is another form of jihad. It has to be undertaken with sincerity and wholeheartedness so that it can reach the heart of the recipient. One should embody a good model in one's own life when inviting others to the path of righteousness.
- Finally, in order to protect the state, sometimes an armed conflict is unavoidable. *Jihād bi'l-Sayf* (Struggle with the Sword) has to be deployed only in the pursuit of a just cause as defined by Allah. This is called *Jihād fī Sabīl Allāh* and can only be pronounced by a duly constituted state authority. It is to be noted that jihad is not just any struggle. It is *Jihād fī Sabīl Allāh* (a struggle in the cause of Allah). This means that the struggle is undertaken with sincerity to gain the pleasure of Allah and not due to any other motive. Thus, it is not undertaken for the acquisition of land or the exploitation of its resources nor is it for the domination of other nations. Jihad must also be pursued while completely abiding by the moral code of behaviour prescribed by the Shariah. The

> pursuance of just war and the administration of justice in war are the reasons for the permissibility of resorting to force. Hence, suicide bombing, acts of terrorism, the murder of innocent people or the assassination of leaders are not sanctioned by Islam nor are they considered to be jihad. Jihad is best understood as a form of sacrifice or struggle, which only resorts to violence when one is attacked, and in which other civilians must not be targeted.

When jihad is restricted to armed conflict and war, which does not affect the daily life of the believers, jihad becomes divorced from day-to-day life. However, jihad is part of one's *Īmān* (faith). All acts of worship train the believer to prepare for jihad (struggle) against his own ego, family, society and, if needs be, his state. This duty is emphasised in several places in the Qur'ān: *O you who believe! Bow down and prostrate yourself before your Lord and serve your Lord and do good that you may prosper. You strive to your utmost* (jihad) *in the cause of Allah in a manner worthy of that striving* (al-Ḥajj: 22–77-78); *As for those who strive (jihad) in Our cause, We shall surely guide them to Our ways, Indeed Allah is with those who do good* (al-ʿAnkabūt 29: 69). It is a great assurance from God that He helps and guides those who strive hard and constantly struggle to follow the path of righteousness. He instructs them how to achieve His good pleasure and shows them the right way.

The other misunderstanding created by some ignorant Muslims is that whatever war Muslims wage is termed jihad.

Not every armed conflict is a jihad unless all the stringent conditions laid down by the Shariah are met. Unfortunately, some people either wilfully or unwittingly exploit the term jihad or mislead others about its true meaning.[30]

## Terrorism

There is a tendency in the media to link Islam with terrorism. It is alleged that the Islamic teachings instigate feelings of extremism which lead to hatred and frustration and then terrorism. This is not a new accusation, as successive western scholars have, for centuries, painted a violent picture of Islam. Despite the enlightenment, secularism and humanism, this image remains part of the cultural mind-set of the West. It is indeed a fact that terrorist activities are taking place all over the world. Yet, it is only the Muslims who are condemned and focused upon. After the tragic event of 11 September 2001, innocent Muslim citizens in the United States and Europe have been harassed, abused and detained without trial. A huge number of Muslims are punished because of the criminal acts of a few individuals. This speaks volumes about the fairness and justice of the champions of human rights in the West.

The Islamic teachings about the sanctity of human life have already been discussed in Chapter II. Killing and terrorising innocent people is categorically forbidden in Islam. Under the Shariah, the punishment for the murder of

[30] Abdur Rashid Siddiqui: *Qur'ānic Keywords: A Reference Guide*. Markfield, Leicester: The Islamic Foundation, 2008, pp. 132-35.

an innocent person is the death penalty. This is because life is absolutely sacred and no one has the right to take it except God, or through the due process of law.

In order to tackle the menace of terrorism, one must try to root out its causes. Mere treatment of the symptoms of terrorism will not help eradicate it. Today, many Muslim countries are ruled by despotic dictators and kings who are corrupt and dishonest. Some sham democracies manipulate the election results by banning and persecuting the opposition. Nearly all regimes are supported by western governments to remain in power. Most western governments have little or no interest in promoting democracy, freedom, justice and the rule of law in these countries, as their only concern is the exploitation of their natural resources and maintaining their hold on these countries. As repression grows and becomes unbearable, disgruntled people take the law into their own hands and retaliate indiscriminately against their rulers and those who support them. There are also many groups that carry out terrorist acts both in the Muslim world and abroad. For example, Israel, which is an Apartheid state, treats the Palestinians worse than they treat animals. Though one cannot approve of any un-Islamic act, the failure of fifty-seven Muslim states to help beleaguered and helpless Muslims is shameful and grossly un-Islamic. This is what leads to the intolerable emergence of many small armed groups that embark on what they call jihad. As part of the Muslim *ummah*, they feel it is their duty to take arms and defend innocent and helpless Muslims facing persecution in different parts of the world as Muslim states are not doing anything despite their enormous resources. Although this is foolhardy and reprehensible, world powers are also tacit collaborators in these acts. In order to eradicate terrorism, justice and fairness in domestic and international affairs must prevail.

## Sectarianism

One of the questions often raised when discussing the introduction of the Shariah in Muslim countries is the existence of different sects among Muslims who disagree on basic issues of *fiqh*. So how can this system work? In reality, there are no more than three or four sects in any one Muslim country. In the world, there are only two major sects: the Sunnis and the Shias. Further sub-divisions of these sects have very minor differences amongst them. Even then, these are schools of thought rather than sects who agree on all fundamental beliefs despite following different schools of *fiqh*.

Sometimes people are dismayed and perturbed by these various schools of *fiqh* and ask why there is not just one system. First of all, it should be understood that all schools are unanimous in their acceptance of the Qur'ān and the Sunnah as the two fundamental sources of the Shariah. There are no differences in *ʿAqā'id* (tenets of faith) and *Muʿāmalāt* (social dealings). There is also agreement on the central core of *ʿIbādah* – only in details are there some differences. On the whole, there is unanimity on almost ninety per cent of all legal matters. Only ten per cent of these matters are the subject of differences, mostly in minor details. These differences are either due to different interpretations of Qur'ānic texts or hadiths or due to the fact that the Prophet performed, at different times, certain acts in different ways. The other reason for such differences is due to *ijtihād*, when there is no guidance available in the Qur'ān or the Sunnah. For example, those Companions who saw the Prophet (peace and blessings be upon him) perform *Ṣalāh* in one way followed the way they saw, while others observed him performing it in a slightly different way and followed it. Thus, whichever way one follows, one is obeying the Prophet (peace and blessings be upon him). The differences point to what is preferred in any given school due to good reasons. These differences show the degree of flexibility within the system. As long as the legal opinion is based on the Qur'ān and the Sunnah, whatever conclusion the *fuqahā'* arrive at deserves to be respected. One has every right to follow what one thinks preferable. Differences therefore are to be tolerated.

There should not be any conflict regarding personal law if it is agreed that the performance of religious rites and customs, as well as the education of the children of each sect, are allowed to follow the interpretation of each sect without any interference from the others. The governance of any country and all its legislations are also decided by the Parliament of that country. When this issue was raised after the independence of Pakistan in 1947, the *'Ulamā'* of all schools of thought debated these matters and unanimously agreed on *Qarār dād-e-Maqāṣid* (Statement of Objectives) which laid down the basic principles of the state of Pakistan.

This was presented by Liaqat Ali Khan, Prime Minister of Pakistan, on 7 March 1949 to the Constituent Assembly and was later incorporated in the country's Constitution. Thus, differences in *fiqh* are not an obstruction to the introduction of the Shariah.

## Theocracy

The introduction of the Shariah often raises the apprehension that this will lead to the establishment of a theocratic state in which all powers are in the hands of a few religious leaders. This impression is created because of the very bitter experience which Europe suffered at the hand of the papacy during the medieval period. There was also a period of inquisition when sectarian groups hunted down heretics and imposed harsh punishments on them.

A theocracy is a system in which the clergy exercise political power or is ruled by someone who has a religious authority or a Divine right. An Islamic state, however, is based on the sovereignty of God even if the power of governance is in the hands of the elected representatives of the people. It is closer to democracy than to theocracy. This can be verified by looking at the early Islamic history. The first four Caliphs were elected by the people, but unfortunately this was replaced later by monarchy even though the title of Caliph continued to be used.

An Islamic state governed by the Shariah is totally different from any theocratic system. It is based on the principle of *Shūrā* (consultation). It treats all human beings as equal and no one has any superiority over others on the basis of colour, race or lineage. The leadership is elected by the people. It is accountable for its actions to the people. All affairs are conducted in a democratic way. No rigidity or obstructions are placed in the way of progress as the Shariah has the mechanism of *ijtihad* which possesses flexibility to meet the changing needs of society.

Theocracies generally do not tolerate freedom of expression and, therefore, no dissenting opinion is allowed. This often leads to the widespread abuse of basic human rights. In Islam, every person is free to have his own views as long as he does not cause dissension.

CHAPTER 5

# THE PROCESS OF IMPLEMENTING THE SHARIAH

The Shariah provides basic guidance regarding all aspects of human life. There is no important aspect of life about which the Shariah has not provided essential and basic guidance. It is instructive to study how this is operated in practice and enforced in society.

## The Shariah in Personal Life

The basis of faith (*īmān*) is man's inner relationship with his Lord. It is based on man's sense of responsibility and accountability to God and knowing that Allah is Omnipresent and watching over his private and public actions. Allah is also aware of man's inner feelings. This pervasive presence of Allah creates God-consciousness. It is love for God and the sense of accountability to Him that motivates man to worship and obey Him and also deters him from transgressing the limits laid down by the Shariah. Inner motivation is the main anchor which keeps the believer on the right path. Institutions, such as the family, society and the state, further reinforce people's adherence to the prescribed limits. Much has been made of the punishments specified by the Shariah but, in fact, these play a lesser vital role. From historical evidence, one can see that the Shariah has been able to command an unparalleled following down the ages and has also been adhered to throughout the world.[31]

## The Shariah's Enforcement in Society and State

As we have seen, it is the individual's willingness to obey that makes him abide by the Shariah's regulations. Similarly, unless society and the state are voluntarily prepared to implement the Shariah, it will not be successfully enforced. It is not possible to bring about change in society by force. A natural and gradual process of change has to be followed.

## Examples from the Prophet's Life (pblessings be upon him)

The best example in this respect is the change that the Prophet (peace and blessings be upon him) effected in Arab society. He did this gradually by replacing some of the existing rules

---

[31] Khurram Murad: Shari'ah: *The Way to God*. Leicester: The Islamic Foundation, 1981, pp. 12-13.

and customs which were introduced by ʿAmr ibn Luḥayy into the Shariah of Prophets Ibrāhīm and Ismāʿīl (peace be upon them) and retained those customs which were inherited by the children of Ismāʿīl.[32] In this way, and for the thirteen long years he spent in Makkah, he invited people to accept Islam's basic beliefs and moral code. And over the years, a group of people accepted Islam. In Madinah, when the Prophet (peace and blessings be upon him) acquired political power, he brought about changes by introducing reforms gradually. It took him another ten years to transform a pagan society into a Muslim *ummah*. The study of the Qur'ān and hadiths clearly demonstrates how this change was brought about. The law of inheritance as mentioned in *Surah al-Nisā'* was revealed in 3 A.H. and laws about marriage were gradually completed in 7 A.H. Laws governing the state, society and mutual relations were revealed piecemeal until 8 A.H., when the prohibition of wine was enforced. Usury was finally prohibited in 9 A.H. Thus, the Prophet (peace and blessings be upon him) did not dismantle the old system instantly upon the establishment of his state in Madinah, although he had the absolute power to do so. Instead, he designed the whole edifice and structure of the state and executed it cautiously at a moderate pace guided by God.[33]

---

32 Shah Waliullah: *The Conclusive Argument from God: Shah Wali Allah of Delhi's Ḥujjat Allāh al-Bālighah*. Translated by Marcia K. Hermansen. Islamabad: Islamic Research Institute, 1996, p. 361.

33 Sayyid Abul 'Alā Mawdūdī: *Islamic Law and Constitution*. Translated and edited by Khurshid Ahmad. Lahore: Islamic Publications, 2005 and Muhammad Asad: *The Principles of State and Government in Islam*. Berkeley: University of California Press, 1961.

Let us now turn to how the prohibition of wine was introduced step-by-step. The first mention of intoxicants happened in a Makkan *Surah, al-Naḥl*: *And out of the fruits of date-palm and grapes you derive intoxicants as well as wholesome sustenance* (16:67). There is a subtle hint of disapproval here that wine is not a wholesome beverage. Later on, in the earlier Madinian period around 2 A.H., the following verse was revealed: *They ask you about wine and games of chance. Say: 'In both these there is great evil, even though there was some benefit for people, but their evil is greater than their benefit'* (*al-Baqarah* 2: 219). Consequently, those who were wise enough stopped drinking and gambling immediately. The third revelation came as a result of an incident when someone who was praying while drunk misread verses from the Qur'ān. It was then that this injunction came around 5 A.H.: *Believers! Do not draw near to the Prayers while you are intoxicated, until you know what you are saying* (al-Nisā' 3: 43). As the prayers during the day come at frequent intervals, people could only drink at night but many people stopped drinking altogether. The complete ban on drinking came a few years later in *Surah* al-Mā'idah: *Believers! Intoxicants, games of chance, idolatrous sacrifices at altars and divining arrows are all abominations, the handiwork of Satan. So turn wholly away from it that you may attain true success. By intoxicants and games of chance Satan only desires to create enmity and hatred among you, and turn you away from remembrance of Allah and from Prayer. Will you not, then, desist?* (5: 90-1).

It is reported that, when these verses were announced, those who were drinking threw away their wine glasses and their tubs of wine were drained voluntarily in the streets of Madinah. Commenting on the wisdom of this gradual introduction of the prohibition of intoxicants, *Umm al-Mu'minīn* ʿĀ'ishah said that had these verses been revealed earlier than they were, not many would have complied with this injunction. It is also worth noting that the Prophet (peace and blessings be upon him) acted himself upon what he commanded others to do. He refrained from any acts which may have caused misunderstanding and confusion among his Companions or given a chance to his enemies to exploit and thus undermine his state. The Companions did not hesitate to seek clarifications about the Prophet's commands or actions whenever they were not sure about something. The following hadith illustrates his wisdom in dealing with such issues. It is narrated by *Umm al-Mu'minīn* ʿĀ'ishah that she asked the Prophet (peace and blessings be upon him) whether al-Ḥaṭīm (a semi-circular enclosure on one side of the Kaʿbah) was part of the House of Allah. He replied: 'Yes, it is.' She asked: 'Then why is it not included in it?' The Prophet (peace and blessings be upon him) said: 'Your nation was short of money.' She then asked: 'Why is the door of the Kaʿbah so high?' The Prophet (peace and blessings be upon him) replied: 'Your people did this in order to allow whomsoever they liked [to enter it] and stop whomsoever they wanted [from entering it]. Your people were living in a state of ignorance until recently and if I were to (demolish the Kaʿbah and) rebuild it, I would include al-Ḥaṭīm in it and make the door at the ground level. But I am afraid that their hearts will revolt (against Islam)' (Bukhārī).[34] This clearly shows that even lawful acts may not be done for the sake of the greater interest of the *ummah*.

## Development of the Islamic Legal System

It may be instructive, in this context, to study how the Islamic legal system developed gradually over the centuries. Companions such as the first four Caliphs and ʿAbdullāh ibn Maʿsūd, ʿAbdullāh ibn ʿAbbās, ʿAbdullāh ibn ʿUmar, *Umm al-Mu'minīn* ʿĀʾishah, and others, who were experts in Islamic jurisprudence laid down the ground rules for the development of the Islamic legal system. Jurists, such as Imam Abū Ḥanīfah (699-767) and his disciples (Imam Abū Yūsuf (d.798) and Imam Muhammad (750-805)), Imam Mālik (711-795) and Imam Shāfiʿī (767-820) were instrumental in building the entire system of Islamic law (*fiqh*) on the basis of the Qur'ān and the Sunnah.

Their students continued to refine and expand this legal system. This does not mean that, during this period, people were rigidly following just one school of *fiqh*. By the 4 century AH (9 CE), the four well-known schools of *fiqh* reached their peak due to political and administrative factors and also because of the expansion of the Muslim population throughout different parts of the world. *Taqlīd*

---

[34] Mohammad Najataullah Siddiqui: *Maqāṣid-e-Sharīʿah*. Islamabad: Idārah Taḥqīqāt-e-Islāmī, 2009, p. 33.

(strict following of one school of *fiqh*) became then widely prevalent. For several centuries, the development of Islamic law remained stagnant.[35] The matter was exacerbated further with the sack of Baghdad by the Mongol armies in 1258 and the abolition of the Abbasid rule. However, Aḥmad Taqī al-Dīn Ibn Tamiyyah (1263-1328), born just five years after the Tatar invasion, challenged the rigidity of *taqlīd*. Though he was a Ḥanbalī like his forefathers, and most of the legal opinions he gave conformed to that School, he did not follow the Ḥanbalī School exclusively. He championed the cause of *ijtihād* for those who have the knowledge and ability to exercise it. In some matters, particularly divorce, he disagreed with all four schools of *fiqh*. However, he did not seek to destroy or discard the valuable work done by earlier jurists nor did he favour showing disrespect to earlier Imams.[36] He was a gifted and prolific writer and authored hundreds of books and treatises on the Islamic sciences, comparative religion, logic and mysticism. His *Majmūʿ al- Fatāwā al-Kubrā* (Compendium of Legal Rulings) on questions put to him, which he answered in writing, runs into thirty-seven large volumes.[37] This Compendium covers many issues including *ʿaqīdah*, *fiqh*, *uṣūl*, hadith, *tafsīr*,

[35] Syed Abul Hasan Ali Nadwi: *Ijtimāʿi Ijtihād*. New Delhi: Ifa Publications, 2010, p. 17.

[36] Syed Abul Hasan Ali Nadwi: *Shaikh-ul-Islam Ibn Taimiyah: Life and Achievements*. Leicester: UK Islamic Academy, 2005, p. 50.

[37] Adil Salahi: *Pioneers of Islamic Scholarship*. Markfield, leicester: The Islamic Foundation, 2006, p. 189.

astronomy, logic, medicine, the Arabic language, geography, history, spirituality, etc.

His pioneering work was continued by his able disciples, particularly Shams al-Dīn Abū Bakr Ibn Qayyim al-Jawziyyah (1292-1350), who remained attached to his mentor, even when the latter was in prison, until his death. Ibn Qayyim was an eminent scholar in his own right and his works are even more refined in their presentation than his master's. He also wrote extensively on all Islamic topics. His book *I'lām al-Muwaqq'īn 'an Rabb al-'Ālamīn* is an encyclopaedic masterpiece in four volumes, which also contains detailed explanations of *Ijtihād* and Consensus and provides a minefield of information for the *fuqahā'* and scholars of hadith and *fatāwā*.[38]

A pioneering effort was made in India during the reign of the Mughal Emperor Aurangzeb, known as 'Ālamgīr (1618-1707), who wanted to codify Islamic law. He gathered about five hundred jurists from India and other Muslim countries to work on this project. The result of this collective work, which is known as *Fatāwā 'Ālamgīrī*, served as the primary source for the Islamic code of law in Mughal territories. This thirty-volume work consists of an exhaustive number of possible scenarios and their juristic rulings by the great Ḥanafī jurists of that time. One of the compilers of this legal encyclopaedia was Shāh 'Abd al-Raḥīm, the father of Shāh Walīullāh (1703-1762), the famous scholar of India.

---

[38] Syed Abul Hasan Ali Nadwi: *Tārīkh-e-Daw'at wa 'Azīmat*. Karachi: Majlis Nashriyat-e-Islam, 1976, p. 381.

This legal code was later replaced by the English legal system when India fell under British rule.[39]

During the 19 century, the Ottoman Caliphate wanted to codify Islamic law in order to update its system of governance. For this purpose, a committee was set up which eventually produced, in 1869, what is known as *Majallat al-Aḥkām al-ʿAdliyyah,* which is based on the Ḥanafī School of law. It is divided into sixteen sections and contains 1851 articles dealing with civil law. This came into force in 1876 through an edict issued by Sultan ʿAbd al-Ḥamīd II (1842-1918). This was later scrapped when Mustafa Kemal (1881-1938) came to power in 1921.[40]

During the last century, many Muslim intellectuals proposed the re-structuring and codification of an Islamic constitution and laws to make them suitable for adoption by Muslim countries. Intellectuals like Muhammad Iqbal (1877–1938) in his *The Reconstruction of the Religious Thought in Islam*[41] suggested ways and means to operationalise Islamic law through a process of legislation in a democratic system. He also wanted to write a book on *ijtihād* and prepared some preliminary notes but could not complete it. Another notable intellectual luminary was Muhammad Asad (1900–1992) –

39 Absar ʿAlam: *Fatāwā ʿĀlamgīrī* in *Chirāgh-e- Rah*, Vol. 12 (6) 1958. *Islāmī Qānūn,* Vol. 1, pp. 399–413.

40 S.S. Onar: *Mujallah-e-Aḥkām-e-ʿAdlīyah per ek Naẓar* in op. cit., pp. 414–422.

41 Muhammad Iqbal: *The Reconstruction of the Religious Thought in Islam*. Lahore, 1930.

formerly Leopold Weiss, an Austrian Jewish convert – wrote extensively in the 1940s on the Islamic system of governance in his magazine *Arafat* and authored a book entitled *The Principles of State and Government in Islam.*[42] In this context, the contribution of Sayyid Abul A'lā Mawdūdī (1903–1979), who was a great thinker and leader of the Islamic Movement in Pakistan, is exceptional. For over more than two decades, he wrote many books, pamphlets and articles elucidating various issues such as the political viewpoint of Islam, the sources of the Islamic constitution, the basis of the Islamic state, the rights of non-Muslims, social justice, legislation and *ijtihād*. These were later collected by Prof. Khurshid Ahmad and published in a book entitled *Islamī Riyāsat* in 1962.[43] Prof. Khurshid Ahmad also translated some articles and papers of Mawlānā Mawdūdī into English and published them in a book entitled *Islamic Law and Constitution*. There were other scholars such as Mawlana Amīn Aḥsan Iṣlāḥī (1904–1997), Dr. Mustafa Ahmad Al-Zarqa (1904–1999), Muhammad Abū Zahrah (1898–1974) and Wahbah Muṣṭafā al-Zuḥaylī (1932–2015) who have also produced valuable literature in this field. The Islamic Council of Europe has also produced two important documents relevant to this effort: *The Universal Declaration of Islamic Human Rights* and *A Model Islamic Constitution.*

---

[42] Muhammad Asad: *The Principles of State and Government in Islam*. Berkeley: University of California Press, 1961, p. 139.

[43] Sayyid Abul 'Alā Mawdūdī: *Islāmī Riyāsat*. Lahore: Islamic Publications Ltd, 1962.

## Introduction of the Islamic Legal System

As mentioned above, the Shariah is a comprehensive code of life. It is the duty of every Muslim to follow the directives of the Shariah in matters such as the acts of worship. Even if one lives in non-Muslim countries, one can still adhere to Muslim personal laws as laid down by the Shariah in matters relating to marriage, divorce and inheritance. In certain non-Muslim countries, such as India and Sri Lanka, Muslim personal laws have been recognised by these countries' parliaments and, as result, Muslims are able to apply them in their personal lives. However, the implementation of the Shariah and its legal and judicial administration at the state level can only be executed by an Islamic State. There are about fifty-seven Muslims countries around the world. Many had been under colonial rule for centuries. The colonial powers had gradually dismantled the Islamic legal system and replaced it by European legal codes. Some Muslim countries later replaced the laws based on the Shariah with the Swiss or German codes of law. But there is now in some Muslim countries popular demand for the introduction of the Shariah. Though these calls may be sincere, formidable obstacles must be surmounted to achieve this goal.

The first of these obstacles is that most Muslim rulers do not want to adopt the Islamic legal system. Some cosmetic measures have been undertaken in some Muslim countries, such as including a clause in their constitutions that no law contrary to the Qur'ān and the Sunnah shall be enacted. But deep down, there is no real political will for the implementation of the Shariah. The second obstacle lies in the fact that years of preparation are needed to educate and train the necessary manpower to run and manage a new Islamic system. The Muslim masses who are emotionally attached to Islam will need to be transformed. This means that they must understand their responsibilities and be ready to perform their duties both in their personal and social lives. Unfortunately, Muslim politicians do not have the foresight to change the system of education in order to produce eminent scholars and the workforce necessary for the implementation of the Islamic legal system.

The final obstacle is that it is not possible to bring about change in society by force. Change has to follow the natural process of happening gradually. Thus, a consistent and gradual process of preparation and hard work is required by all sections of the Muslim *ummah* for the introduction of the Shariah. Sadly, neither the Muslim masses nor their leaders are ready and willing to undertake this difficult task. The Qur'ān has aptly observed: *He did not venture to scale the steep and difficult path* (al-Balad 90: 11). Muslim scholars have done a tremendous job in preparing the plan, structure and outline of an Islamic constitution for modern times. But these cannot be implemented unless there is a sincere political will to follow the Shariah by the leaders of Muslim countries.

CHAPTER 6

# FIQH AL-AQALLIYYĀT (ISLAMIC JURISPRUDENCE FOR MINORITIES)

## Introduction

It is estimated that nearly half of the Muslim population of the world now lives as a minority in non-Muslim countries. Muslims are the largest minority in India (177 million or 14.6per cent of the whole population). India has more Muslims than any other country in the world, apart from Indonesia and Pakistan. After World War II, sizeable Muslim populations were established in Western Europe and North America.

In countries where Muslims represent a minority and are not, therefore, under the rule of a Muslim government, they may face particular problems that need solving in order to live according to the Islamic teachings. The residence of Muslims in non-Muslim countries has many implications from the Shariah's point of view. Many classical jurists disapproved of Muslims living for long periods of time in countries which are termed *dār al-kufr* (abode of unbelief). The reason for their proscription is that Muslims may not be able to freely practise their religion and this may lead them to compromise their Islamic duties. Today, the vast majority of Muslim jurists are of the opinion that it is permissible for Muslims to reside in non-Muslims countries without contradicting their faith.[44] Many contemporary jurists consider these non-Muslim countries as *dār al-ʿahd* (abode of covenant) where Muslims may live in contractual obligations with these countries. These non-Muslim countries can also be considered as *dār al-amān* (abode of peace) or *dār al-daʿwah* (abode of dawah) and compare them to the Makkan period during which the Muslims bore witness to their faith, although they were a minority in society.

The role of the Shariah has always been to provide solutions for the problems faced by Muslims and answer their needs rather than create hardship for them. *Fiqh* is different from the Shariah in that sense: the Shariah refers to the revealed religion as a whole while *fiqh* refers to how the rules of the Shariah are applied from the jurists' points of view. There are many differences between the conditions of Muslims living

---

44 Andrew F. March: *Islam and Liberal Citizenship: The searching of an Overlapping Consensus*. Oxford: Oxford University Press, 2009, p. 104.

as minorities in non-Muslim countries and Muslims living in Muslim countries. When issuing legal rulings, *fiqh* always takes into consideration the differences in time and place. *Fiqh* is, in its very nature, mainly concerned with finding solutions to people's problems and making their life easy within the ambit of the Shariah. Muslim scholars did realise that Muslim minorities deserve a new legal discipline to address their unique religious needs. *Fiqh al-Aqalliyyāt* (Islamic jurisprudence for minorities) was developed as a means of assisting these Muslim minorities. As Taha Jabir Alalwani has observed: 'the role of Muslims in their new homeland, their relationship to the world Muslim community, the future of Islam outside its present borders and how it may go forward to establish its universality in all parts of the globe are the issues which have to be tackled with a fresh juristic vision, based on the principles, objectives and higher values of the Qur'ān in conjunction with aims of the Shariah. A new methodology for replicating the Prophet's example is needed in order to make his way clearer and more accessible to everyone at all times.'[45]

On this basis, contemporary jurists have argued that the distinguishing feature of Islam is providing ease. The Qur'ān and the Sunnah emphasise that the *dīn* should never become a burden. There are several verses that reiterate this message: *Allah wants ease and not hardship for you* (al-Baqarah 2: 185); *Allah wants to lighten your burdens, for man is created weak* (al-Nisā' 4: 28); *Allah does not want to lay any hardship*

---

[45] Taha Jabir Alalwani: *Towards a Fiqh for Minorities: Some Basic Reflections*. London: International Institute of Islamic Thought, 2010, pp. 6-7.

*upon you* (al-Mā'idah 5: 6); *He has not laid any hardship in religion* (al-Ḥajj 22: 78).

The Prophet (peace and blessings be upon him) repeated this message several times through his advice and practice. He said: 'The best part of your *dīn* is the one that is easiest' (Aḥmad and Bukhārī in *al-Adab al-Mufrad*). It is reported by *Umm al-Mu'minīn* 'Ā'ishah that whenever the Prophet (peace and blessings be upon him) had to choose between two options, he always chose the one that was easiest unless it was unlawful. If the easiest option was unlawful, then he always avoided it (Bukhārī and Muslim). The Prophet (peace and blessings be upon him) said: 'Allah loves that the dispensations He has given be followed just as He dislikes the commission of sins' (Aḥmad and Bayhaqī).

In view of the guidance given above, Sheikh Yusuf al-Qaradawi, in a meeting of the European Council of Fatwa and Research held in Dublin in 2003, said that, according to his analysis, the provision of ease, the removal of hardship and progression in the implementation of injunctions were the predominant parts of *fiqh* during the time of the Prophet (peace and blessings be upon him). After the period of the Companions, people became cautious and, then, they closed all doors of ease due to prudence. Now the right course of action for Muslims today is to revert to the path of the earlier period of the *ummah*.[46] The *fiqh* for Muslim minorities should

---

46 Islamopediaonline.org/websites-institutions/european-council-fatwas-and-research-dublin-ireland and Salahuddin Sultan: *Fiqh al-Aqalliyyāt: Tā'aruf, Uṣūl awr Taṭbīq*. New Delhi: Ifa Publications, 2012, p. 81.

not remain rigid or restricted; it should rather be debated and be the subject of *ijtihād*. The solution to the problems should not be based on expediency or exceptionality. It is essential that a group of experts with different specialisations come together under the auspices of some authoritative body to discuss the issues thoroughly. Should a question of a political, economic, ethical or medical nature arise, specialists from all disciplines should jointly examine the religious and social aspects of the issue. This arrangement would be more effective than if it were left to Shariah experts alone.[47]

## The Role and Duties of Muslims

The prime duty of Muslims is to preserve their faith and identity wherever they may be. It is much easier to maintain these when one lives in a Muslim environment. Muslims should therefore safeguard their Islamic faith and identity as the Qur'ān reminds: *and do not die save in submission to Allah* (Āl ʿImrān 3: 102). The other important duty is to transmit the Islamic faith and culture to the next generations of Muslims as Allah commands, *Believers, guard yourself and your families from a fire* (al-Taḥrīm: 66: 6).

The Qur'ān has prescribed a role for the Muslims regardless of their number in the community they live in. This role is to command good and forbid evil (3: 110). This also includes witness unto mankind (2: 143 and 22: 78), which

[47] Taha Jabir Alalwani: *Towards a Fiqh for Minorities: Some Basic Reflections*, 2010, pp. 37-38.

means that the *ummah* is required to convey the message of Islam to the rest of mankind. Muslims cannot be absolved from this duty whatever the circumstances. While living among non-Muslims, it is more important that Muslims should save their fellow human beings from accountability in the Hereafter. This was precisely the duty performed in Makkah by the Prophet (peace and blessings be upon him) and his Companions. *Daʿwah* may not have been the prime reason for those Muslims who migrated to non-Muslim countries. But since they have chosen to live in non-Muslim countries, they might as well make it worthwhile by doing *daʿwah* work. They should develop a rapport with the host community. But before doing so, they should be informed about Islamic beliefs and practices and try to dispel the ignorance and prejudice prevalent in the West about Islam and Muslims. They have to be forthcoming and reach out to society. Remaining in isolation and concentrating themselves in ghettos will only perpetuate prejudices against them.

## Social Obligations

As Muslims have made non-Muslim countries their home and are given permission to stay, they have entered into a binding contract to live peacefully in these countries and to contribute to the wellbeing of their societies. They have to abide by the laws of the countries in which they live. They may not approve of all these countries' laws but they must not wilfully violate them. Instead, they can lobby to change the laws they disprove of. There may even be a few laws and regulations which interfere with the performance of their religious duties. These have to be negotiated and resolved with tact and sagacity.

Muslims should live as good citizens and not abuse the privileges they are afforded. Their non-Muslim neighbours should feel secure and safe from them and their presence should cause no concerns for others. The Prophet (peace and blessings be upon him) said: 'By God! He is not a true believer, he from whose mischief his neighbours are not safe' (Bukhārī and Muslim). Muslims should be actively involved in preserving the peace and quiet of their neighbourhoods. They should participate in social and cultural activities that do not conflict with Islamic teachings.

There are several Prophetic traditions which provide guidance about Muslims' relations with their neighbours whether they are Muslim or people of other faiths. The Prophet (peace and blessings be upon him) is also reported to have said that Jibrīl constantly reminded him about the rights of neighbours so much so that he feared that neighbours would be included in the category of those entitled to one's inheritance. It is reported that ʿAbdullāh ibn ʿUmar once slaughtered a goat and asked that some of its meat be shared with his Jewish neighbour. He mentioned that the Prophet (peace and blessings be upon him) encouraged them to have good relations with their neighbours. Good relations with them include greeting them, exchanging gifts with them, sharing food, looking after the sick amongst them and attending their funerals. Helping neighbours in need and spending money on them is also a form of *ṣadaqah* (benevolent acts for which there is a reward from Allah).

According to Islamic teachings, spending in the way of Allah (*infāq fi sabīl Allāh*) should not be restricted to Muslims only. Helping all human beings, regardless of their faith, is the duty of all believers. It is particularly necessary for Muslims to help the victims of natural or man-made disasters in any part of the world. There are in *Surah al-Baqarah* extensive passages which encourage Muslims to spend their wealth on the needy and the disadvantaged members of society regardless of their faith.

**Participation in Political Activities**

In 2004, an international seminar organised in Hyderabad by the Islamic Fiqh Academy, India, was attended by over thirty scholars from around the world. This seminar discussed some of the important problems facing Muslims living in non-Muslim countries. The majority of participants agreed that it is permissible for Muslims to participate in elections through putting themselves forward as candidates, campaigning for others and voting. They argued that such participation has many beneficial religious interests for the *ummah*. If Muslims were not to participate in the decision-making bodies of their respective countries, their views and interests will not be properly represented. They also emphasised the importance of voting which is a sort of *amānah* (trust), recommendation and consultation. From the Islamic point of view, Muslims should perform the duty of trust and give the right advice when consulted.[48] In this respect, a historical precedent was presented to support this view from the conduct of the Prophet Yūsuf (peace be upon him) when he was appointed for an important ministerial post in Egypt. According to Imam al-Rāzī, the Prophet Yūsuf (peace be upon him) provided his services for the benefit of common people and safeguarded their interests. Accepting a ministerial position in a non-Muslim government is therefore permissible.[49] Similarly, the migration of the Prophetic Companions to Abyssinia (modern Ethiopia) and their residence there, during the time of the Prophet (peace and blessings be upon him), provided a precedent for living in a non-Muslim country and participating in its social and political affairs.[50]

## Obligations towards the Wider *Ummah*

The Qur'ān declares that the believers are brothers (49: 10). This bond of brotherhood is also emphasised in several Prophetic sayings. In one hadith, they are described as different parts of the same body, such that when one of its parts aches, the whole body feels discomfort (Bukhārī and Muslim).

---

48 *Ghair Muslim Mumālik me Ābād Muslamānū ke khuch Aham Mas'āl* (Some Important Problems of Muslims Living in Non-Muslim Countries). New Delhi: Ifa Publications, 2010, pp. 53-68.

49 As quoted in Sultan Ahmed Islahi: *Musalmān Aqlliyatun kā Maṭlūba Kirdār* (The Desired Role of Muslim Minorities) Azamgarh: Fikr-o-Āgahi, 1988, pp. 128-130.

50 op. cit., pp. 139-147.

Living as minorities in non-Muslim countries, the responsibility of Muslims will be determined by the laws and treaties which govern their stay. Most states are members of the United Nations and are signatories to many international conventions and treaties which make their citizens bound by the regulations of these conventions and treaties. The best way to help oppressed Muslims in other countries is therefore by making effective representations on their behalf in international and regional forums and providing emergency help through relief organisations and international agencies.

In the light of the above discussion, it is imperative for Muslim minorities to have good relations with their host communities. Historically, Islam has tried to assimilate the local culture when it did not conflict with Islamic teachings. From Indonesia to Morocco, there is a diversity of cultures. In time, there will also be a European and British Islamic culture.

Muslims who have made Britain their home face many challenges and hurdles. These can only be met by being conscious of their Islamic and cultural heritage. They can face these challenges by adopting Islamic values themselves and by seeing that their houses are in order. By following the path of *da'wah* they will be safeguarding their societies.

CHAPTER 7

# CONCLUSION

It is hoped that the basic concepts, objectives and framework of the Shariah have been clearly explained in the previous chapters. Whatever reservation one may have about any specific Shariah provision, it is still possible to appreciate that its objective is to create a humane, fair and peaceful society, which is a blessing for mankind. But how does the Shariah distinguish itself and its value system from the prevailing secular systems? Let us turn here to the Shariah's unique characteristics which are highlighted below:

- Unlike other systems, the Shariah is given by God, the Creator, the Most Merciful, the Most Just. Hence, its guidance and teachings are based on Divine knowledge, wisdom and justice and does not favour any particular segment of society as it is strictly impartial. It is unfair to judge it by man's own limited knowledge, experience, criteria and standards. The One, Who has created, knows best what is beneficial and harmful to His creation.

The guidance of the Shariah is comprehensive and covers all aspects of a person's life. There is no dichotomy between the sacred and the secular, as man is composed of body and soul. The Shariah guides man to the right path so as to achieve success both in this world and in the Hereafter. This characteristic of the Qur'ān is mentioned thus: *We sent down the Book to you which makes everything clear, and serves as a guidance and mercy and glad tidings to those who have submitted to Allah* (al-Naḥl 16: 89).

- The Shariah is balanced and moderate. It strikes a balance between the needs of the body and the needs of the soul; between the intellect and emotions; between life in this world and life in the Hereafter. It caters for the needs of the individual and his duty to the family, community and humanity. It promotes piety yet prohibits monasticism. The Prophet (peace and blessings be upon him) advised his Companions who desired to lead an ascetic way of life, saying: 'Your body has a right on you, your eyes have a right on you, your family has a right on you and your guest has a right on you' (Bukhārī). These rights should therefore not be ignored while engaging in voluntary prayers, fasting and night vigils. In this respect, it is noteworthy that the Qur'ān designates the Muslims as *Ummatan Wasaṭan* (the community of the middle-way). Explaining the meaning of this expression, Mawlānā Mawdūdī wrote:

> The Arabic expression which way be translated as 'the community of the middle-way' is too rich in meaning to find an adequate equivalent in any other language. It signifies that distinguished group of people which follow the path of justice and equity, of balance and moderation; a group which occupies a central position among the nations of the world so that its relationship with all of them is based on righteousness and justice and none receives its support in wrong and injustice.[51]

- One important attribute of the Shariah is that it has made things easy for human beings. Some religions fetter their adherents by undue restrictions in the observation of worship, consumption of food and other formalities relating to daily life. The Qur'ān refers to this in *Surah al-A'rāf* wherein it is mentioned that Allah has sent a Prophet of mercy (peace and blessings be upon him), who is mentioned in the Torah and the Gospel which are in the hands of the

51 Sayyid Abul A'lā Mawdūdī: *Towards Understanding the Qur'ān: An abridged version of Tafhīm al-Qur'ān*. Markfield, Leicester: The Islamic Foundation, 2006, p. 40.

People of the Book and this Prophet commands what is good and forbids what is evil and *he (the Prophet) makes the clean things lawful to them and prohibits all corrupt things and removes from them their burdens and the shackles that were upon them* (7: 157). Thus, those who believe in him and follow the guidance he brought shall prosper.

Similarly, the Prophet (peace and blessings be upon him) said: 'Allah did not make me someone who makes things difficult for others, but he sent me as a teacher who makes things easy' (Muslim).

This ease and facility is available in the individual's performance of the acts of worship as well as in his daily life. The Shariah provides concessions in certain special circumstances in both private and public life. There is permission to do *tayammum* (dry ablution) instead of *wuḍū'* (ritual ablution) when water is not available. Prayers can be shortened and combined when travelling. They can also be performed while sitting down or lying down when one is too sick to stand or sit. It is also permissible not to fast while travelling or when one is sick or too old.

- One of the unique characteristics of the Shariah is its adaptability. Some segments of the Shariah are immutable, such as the basic beliefs and the acts of worship. *Ijtihād* (juristic reasoning) is used by expert jurists to accommodate social changes in order to keep abreast with the changing needs of society without violating the clear injunctions of the Shariah.

In this way, the Shariah strikes a fine balance between continuity and change.

- The Shariah brings about social change and reform gradually. Islamic law favours realistic reform and is against change through revolutionary means. The Prophet (peace and blessings be upon him) did not take sweeping actions even with regard to right causes for fear that people might reject them. The gradual procession of the Shariah is manifested in the dispensations it provides with regard to fasting and prayers for travellers and the sick.
- Another important aspect of the Shariah is that Allah has preserved and protected its sources. The Qur'ān is exactly the same as when it was first revealed by Allah to His Prophet (peace and blessings be upon him). The Qur'ān states: *We have, without doubt, sent down the Message; and we assuredly will preserve it* (al-Ḥijr 15: 9). Similarly, the traditions of the Prophet (peace and blessings be upon him) were meticulously preserved by Muslim scholars by inventing a whole discipline concerned with scrutinising the authenticity of different traditions to distinguish the sound traditions from those which are weak or fabricated.
- Finally, the Shariah, unlike other man-made systems, is eternal. The Qur'ān, revealed in the Arabic language, has been preserved for the last fourteen centuries without any change. As the Prophet Muhammad (pbuh) is the last in the long chain of messengers,

there will be no more prophets after him. Hence, the guidance provided by the Qur'ān and the Sunnah will remain valid until the end of time. For this reason, the Prophet (peace and blessings be upon him) was sent to all mankind unlike earlier prophets who were sent to specific nations. This is clearly mentioned in the Qur'ān: *(O Prophet!) We have sent you to all humanity as none other than a bearer of good tidings and as a warner. But most people do not know* (Saba' 34: 28).

In sum, we can say that the Shariah is capable of creating a just, peaceful and caring society which will be a great blessing for mankind. One should not be dismayed by the state of Muslim societies which are infested with all kinds of ills and corruption because of neglecting God's code of life. The salvation of Muslims, and indeed the rest of mankind, lies in their return to that invigorating source of guidance: *the* Shariah.

APPENDIX

# THE FUNDAMENTALS OF THE SHARIAH

The Shariah is composed of revealed fundamentals and subsidiaries which are deduced therefrom by human reasoning. Revelation provides the basic raw material of law and fixes boundaries which cannot be transgressed in any case. Within these boundaries human reason has been charged with the sacred obligation to use the raw material provided by the Shariah to promote the supreme values which are the crowning glory of humanity. The life and vitality of Islamic Law, therefore, depend on the dynamic role of human reason which has to be applied in an ever-changing socio-political and cultural context. Thus, it has to act and react to infinitely diverse situations and circumstances, which necessitates constant re-interpretation at different stages of evolution.

All extant treaties and textbooks on Islamic Law and jurisprudence state that there are four sources of Islamic Law. I do not agree. In my opinion, there are just three sources of Islamic Law. Two of them are primary sources that consist of the Holy Qur'ān and the Sunnah of the Prophet (peace and blessings be upon him). They consist, in fact, of what in modern juristic parlance is known as the material source of law. The third source is *ijtihād*. *Ijtihād*, according to Sir Abdul Rahim, is a process of 'exerting oneself to form an opinion in a case or rule of law.'[52] Dr. Muhammad Iqbal has described this principle as '[t]he principle of movement within the structure of Islam.' It involves the operation of human reason, intelligence and intellect in the formation of an independent judgement on legal questions within the parameters fixed by the Qur'ān and the Sunnah. Here, we find the dynamic role of human reason mentioned above. *Ijtihād* is aided and regulated by certain well-defined and distinct modes of applying reason in the light of the above-mentioned primary sources, i.e. the Qur'ān and the Sunnah. These modes of reasoning are represented by certain well-known concepts that may be regarded as the forms, means and instruments of *ijtihād*. A very brief and sketchy outline of this is given as follows:

1. Firstly, there are certain well-recognised principles of exegesis and interpretation, which fix the meaning,

[52] Abdur Rahim: *The Principles of Muhammadan Jurisprudence According to the Hanafi, Maliki, Shafi'i and Hanbali Schools*. London: Luzac, 1911.

explicate, specify, restrict or extend the coverage of the textual sources. These have reference to such principles as (i) *'Ibārat al-Naṣṣ*, (ii) *Ishārat al-Naṣṣ*, (iii) *Dalālat al-Naṣṣ* and (iv) *Iqtiḍā' al-Naṣṣ*. The first of these principles deals with the simple and direct meaning of the text and, as such, refers to the literal or grammatical rule of interpretation. The other three principles indicate three different ways in which the rule of necessary implication can come into play. By the use of these principles of necessary implication hitherto undiscovered meaning of the text can be extrapolated, thus introducing a new interpretation or extending the coverage of the old meanings of the texts.

2. *Qiyās* or analogical deduction, by which a common effective cause or *'Illah* is identified and, thus, a command contained in a text is made applicable to circumstances not directly contemplated or referred to in the text.
3. *Istiḥsān* (juristic preference). This concept is mainly peculiar to Ḥanafī Jurisprudence or *fiqh*. According to Imam Sarakhsī, it is 'the setting aside of analogy *(Qiyās)* and seeking what is more suitable to the people.' This is obviously for promoting public interest and justice, with the view of eliminating rigour, complexity and harsh results arising from *Qiyās*. It is also resorted to where a strict *Qiyās* would lead to abolishing an already existing, salutary, or at least harmless, custom. Ḥanafī jurists use this principle with such frequency that some jurists define *Istiḥsān* as a latent analogy (*Qiyās Khafī*).

4. *Al-Maṣāliḥ al-Mursalah.* It is called *Istiḥsān al-Maṣāliḥ* by Abū Zahrā, *Istidlāl* by Imam al-Ḥarmayn, *al-Istidlāl al-Mursal* by Sarakhsī and *Qiyās ʿĀmm by Mustafa al-Zarqa.* According to Ḥanafis, it is a kind of *Qiyās. Al-Maṣāliḥ al-Mursalah* is a principle by which rules of law are discovered and formulated on the basis of such public expediency, or interest, which is not derived from any *Naṣṣ* of the Qur'ān or Sunnah. In other words, this principle defines and recognises the scope of public policy and interest as a legitimate consideration for the application and enforcement of law.
5. *Istidlāl.* By means of this principle, one thing is inferred from another for the purpose of deducting a rule, but the basis of reasoning is not *'Illah* or effective cause. Thus, it is different from *Qiyās.*
6. *Sadd al-Dharā'i*ʿ. According to this principle, anything that can be a means or a cause of anything unlawful is itself unlawful. Similarly, anything that can be a means or a cause of anything compulsorily ordained is itself ordained. How this principle is applied can be illustrated by the following examples from the Qur'ān and the Sunnah:

    a. Allah Almighty says, *Do not revile those whom they invoke, other than Allah, because they will revile Allah in ignorance out of spite (*Al-Anʿām, 6:108*).* Here something which need not be forbidden is nevertheless forbidden, not for itself but because it can be a means or a cause of something which is undesirable.

b. The Holy Prophet Muhammad (peace and blessings be upon him) did not allow the killing of hypocrites because doing so would have led to a proportionately much greater strategic harm to the cause of Islam. The infidels of Makkah al-Mukarramah would have used this incident to make propaganda that Muhammad (peace and blessings be upon him) was killing his own Companions.

c. The Holy Prophet Muhammad (peace and blessings be upon him) forbade the cutting of hands, a *Ḥadd* punishment, for theft during war-time, although this exception to the general command contained in the *Naṣṣ* of the Holy Book is not found explicitly anywhere in the Qur'ān. However, this course was adopted to prevent the possibility that convicted persons might run away and join hands with the enemy. Thus, we find here an example of the non-performance of an absolute duty commanded by the Qur'ān in exceptional circumstances to avoid a proportionately far greater damage. Imam Ibn al-Qayyim has presented no less than ninety examples of the application of this principle. It has been said: 'One half of Islamic Law is based on the principle of *Sadd al-Dharā'iʿ*.

7. The principle of *Ḍarūrah* or *Iḍṭirār*. This principle provides scope for exceptional behaviour which is dictated by some dire need or necessity. When there is a situation of extreme and dire need or necessity, what is otherwise

totally forbidden and unlawful becomes permitted. But this exceptional suspension of commands and prohibitions can be justifiably resorted to only when dire need or necessity lasts. The principal is based on the maxim: 'Necessity permits forbidden things'.

8. Customs and Usages. *ʿUrf* and *ʿĀdah* are recognised and enforced as rule of law if they are not repugnant to any text-based injunction or value of the Shariah or any speculations agreed upon between parties. They are given the status of an ancillary source of law, and they serve as a means and guide to the determination of meaning, or circumscription of the generality of an injunction. It has been stated in *al-Hidāyah, Bāb al-Ribā,* that in 'matters where there is no explicit injunction, the decision will be made according to the habits and practices of the people. It is the opinion of Imam Abū Yūsuf that in respect of all things that can be exchanged, loaned or sold, customs and usages will be relied upon. In fact, customs and usages are important considerations in all matters that belong to what is called *Muʿāmalāt.*'

However, there are numerous instances where a text-based injunction, *Ḥukm Manṣūṣ,* has its basis in some customs or usages. In such cases, when a custom or usage changes, the text-based injunction will itself undergo a corresponding change, thus an element of considerable flexibility creeps into the corpus of law. This is elucidated by Imam al-Shāmī who, while explaining the opinion of Ibn al-Humām, the author of *Durr al-Mukhtār*, wrote: 'prevalent usage, which is consistent and not opposed to any text-based injunction, is reliable. Measurement by a given standard of four things, and measurement by weight of gold and silver is based on this, which was the usage in the time of the Holy Prophet. Consequently, if the usages had been different, the injunctions of the Holy Prophet would have been different. If the usage had changed during his life time, he would have commanded according to the changed usage. To sum up, the *ʿIllah* or effective cause of the text-based injunction in such cases is usage. Therefore, in respect of it, whatever the time, only usage will be relied upon.'[53]

9. Furthermore, some leading jurists are in agreement that there is some sort of interaction between text-based injunctions and customs and usages. Ibn ʿĀbidīn wrote: 'Usage can specify textual commands of general applicability and allow giving up *Qiyās*.' As an example for this, it is pointed out that, although there is a textual command in the hadith of the Holy Prophet that 'No one should sell that which he does not possess', yet it was not applied in certain cases due to customs and usage. For instance, the purchase of a thing to be made to order (*Bayʿ al-Istiṣnāʿ*) and the purchase of a thing by advance payment *(Bayʿ al-salam)* are in violation of the above hadith. Nevertheless, because this kind of transaction were customary modes, they were

53 Ibn al-Humām: *Durr al-Mukhtar*, vol.4, p. 281.

recognised as legitimate by the Shariah. This is why Ibn 'Ābidīn wrote in his book *Nashr al-'Urf*: 'it is essential for the *Mujtahid* to be familiar with the practices and usages of people. There are many injunctions which undergo change due to changes in the practices of the time.' Ibn 'Ābidīn has further expressed his opinion on the subject quoting fatwas from two famous and pious jurists named al-Kirmānī and al-Ḍāhirī to the effect that 'a jurist who does not know the circumstances of his time is an ignorant being.'[54] The Disorder of the Time (*'Umūm al-Balwā* and *Fasād al-Zamān*). In the enforcement of Islamic injunctions, the Shariah takes into consideration man's temperament and environment as well as his experiences. Therefore, if extreme rigour or a compelling necessity results from the observance of a commandment, or it becomes impossible to escape completely from some evil due to the degeneration of the environment or some other cause, then the jurists either specify the general applicability of the injunction or tackle the ensuing negative aspect, proposing instead a positive aspect, which is the aspect of removing harshness.

When moral or social degeneration become rampant in a society, or the situation is such that acting on a particular Islamic injunction completely and precisely becomes impossible, then it is permissible to circumscribe the general applicability of the textual

---

[54] Ibn 'Ābidīn: *Nashr al-'Urf.*

command, or change the fatwa regarding an injunction which is not text-based (*Manṣūṣ*). This is necessary because it is the intent of the Shariah itself that people should be rescued from rigour and harshness as much as possible. A renowned Muslim jurist has stated that the principle of *ʿUmūm al-Balwā* is applicable to the above-mentioned situation. Imam Ibn al-Qayyim has explained the rationale of this principle as well as that of custom and usage, in his book *al-Ṭuruq al-Ḥukmiyyah,* in the following words: 'The Shariah is based on the wise policies and benefit of the life of this world and that of the Hereafter. It is an embodiment of wisdom and benefit. Any proposition that leads away from justice to tyranny, from mercy to hardship, from benefit to disorder or from wisdom to folly, will not be a proposition of the Shariah, even though it may have been incorporated in the Shariah through interpretation. What is involved here is not violation of the revealed text, but obedience to other revealed texts which happens to be more specific situations and therefore more relevant. Three such texts are mentioned here: *Allah wants ease not hardship for you* (al-Baqarah 2:185); *He (Allah) has chosen you, and He has imposed no hardship in religion* (al-Ḥajj 22:78) and *But none shall be burdened with more than he is able to bear* (al-Baqarah 2:233).'

The object behind the principle of *ʿUmum al-Balwā* and the disorderly state of the time *(Fasād al-Zamān)* is to preserve the Shariah from total breakdown and to maintain its eternal status. In the main, these principles were specific to situations where Muslims are not in a position to have their own constitution and law-making. But in countries where Muslims are in a position to have their own constitution and law-making, the applicability of these principles is limited to international affairs, which include transactions in the field of finance, trade, commerce and international aid. The application of these principles is guided by the weighing of the possibilities of good and evil resulting from them. According to jurists, attempts to eliminate evil can lead to one of four consequences: (1) evil is replaced by good; (2) evil is reduced; (3) an evil is replaced by another evil; (4) an evil is replaced by a greater evil. The elimination of evil is permitted, even commanded, in the first two cases; it is a matter of discretion and judgment involving *ijtihād* in the third case; but it is categorically forbidden in the fourth case.

10. The principle of *Tadrīj* or step-by-step approach. Islam is a *dīn of Fiṭrah* (primordial nature) and *Ḥikmah* (Wisdom). It is significant that Allah Almighty sent His Holy Prophet to mankind not only to teach the Holy Qur'ān but also *Ḥikmah*, which means wisdom or wise policy or strategy. Allah Almighty says in *Surah al-Jummʿah* (62:2): *It is He Who has sent amongst the unlettered a Messenger from among themselves, to rehearse to them His verses, to purify them and to impart to them the Book and the Wisdom.* In line with this wisdom Allah Almighty has Himself favoured

a step-by-step approach. This can be elucidated by a saying from *Umm al-Mu'minīn* 'Ā'ishah (may Allah be pleased with her). She said: 'The first revealed *Surahs* mentioned hell and heaven. Afterwards, when people became firm in Islam, the commandments regarding what is lawful and what is unlawful were revealed. If the commandment against drinking wine were revealed in the very beginning, people would have said, "We will never give up drinking". Similarly, if the prohibition regarding fornication had been revealed at the beginning, people would have refused to give it up.'

Similarly, in his book *al-Mawāfaqāt*, Imam al-Shāṭibī mentions an incident where the young 'Abd al-Mālik remonstrates with Caliph 'Umar ibn 'Abd āl-'Azīz that he was slack in enforcing the commandments of the Shariah. 'Umar ibn 'Abd 'Azīz said in reply, 'Son, do not be impetuous! Allah Almighty condemned the drinking of wine in the Qur'ān twice and then prohibited it on the third time. I am afraid if I were suddenly to impose what is right on people, they would spurn it at once and this would become a permanent problem.' He adopted a similar approach regarding the usurpations committed by the progeny of Marwān. One must remember that 'Umar ibn 'Abd al-'Azīz was highly esteemed for his knowledge of the Shariah, his unwavering dedication to Islam and his extreme piety. Many people reckon that he was among the Rightly-guided Caliphs (*al-Khulafā' al-Rāshidūn*) of Islam. This indicates that when disorder or degeneration becomes the order of the day in a particular society, it is necessary and right to eliminate the disorder or degeneration by undertaking step-by-step measures.

This is how things ought to be because, according to Qur'ānic teachings, even the Islamisation of human personality is a step-by-step affair. According to well-known teachings of the Shariah, there are three distinct stages through which human personality passes: (i) *Islām,* (ii) *Īmān,* and (iii) *Iḥsān.* In addition to these stages of belief, there are numerous stages of non-belief in which the human personality can be involved. In view of this, it is natural and inevitable that human society also undergoes change through a gradual, step-by-step process. Therefore, if one wants to rectify disorder and degeneration, one would do well to keep this aspect of gradual change in mind. If one ignores this, one will only aggravate matters further as ignoring it will only result in *Fitnah* (anarchy and hardship) which is absolutely abhorred by Islam. In this context, one may refer to the Qur'ānic maxim: 'Disorder is more serious than murder'.

11. Last of all, *ijmāʿ*. *Ijmāʿ* means consensus, which is the agreement of the Muslim jurists of a particular age on a question of law. According to Shāh Walīullāh, Abū Bakr al-Rāzī and Ṭabarī, unanimity is not essential for it as it can also be formed by the majority of jurists. It is more important to realise that *ijmāʿ* is not something that contains material of law, nor is it a process of discovery of law. It is a process by which a rule of law

already found, discovered, or arrived at by *ijtihād,* is authenticated or elevated to the status of law. *Ijmā*ʿ, therefore, is not a source of law. It is a name given to the recognised process of authentication of a rule of law already found through different modes of reasoning and instruments of *ijtihād* mentioned above, which are to be applied within the parameters fixed by the Qur'ān and the Sunnah. It is, therefore, true to say that *Qiyās* and other modes of reasoning, mentioned above, regulate and control *ijtihād,* while *ijmā*ʿ authenticates it.

*Ijtihād* and *ijmā*ʿ are complementary and *ijmā*ʿ has to operate in combination with *ijtihād.* This combination may be called the '*ijmā*ʿ*-ijtihād* Process'. The *ijmā*ʿ*-ijtihād* process can justifiably be described as Islam's early counterpart and substitute, albeit in an embryonic form, of the modem process of legislation. In fact, modern legislation is nothing but an *ijmā*ʿ*-ijtihād* process conducted through chosen representatives of the *ummah* in a given Islamic country. It is important to add that no mode of reasoning or *ijmā*ʿ process can be used to overstep, disregard, negate, violate or abrogate any text of the Qur'ān or the Sunnah of the Holy Prophet or the general spirit and objectives of the Shariah. Contrary to the misconception prevailing in some quarters, the scope of legislation in Islam is far from limited or negligible. When one says that Islam is a completely perfect *dīn,* one does not mean that it contains pre-fabricated, once-for-all solutions for each and every future problem. This would be totally unrealistic because the commands and injunctions of the Shariah are unavoidably limited, whereas facts, situations and circumstances and future problems, to which these commands and injunctions are meant to apply, are infinite.

The use of *ijtihād* and *ijmāʿ* must strictly adhere to the well-known guiding principles, fundamental values and norms of Islam. These must permeate and run as life-blood in the body of the entire legal and social system. In this way, the continuity of the essence, identity and spirit of the Shariah is maintained, yet dealing with any challenge that the future may bring remains possible. This is done through the *ijmāʿ-ijtihād* process, mentioned above, which helps in the task of legislation. Thus, contrary to some misconceptions prevalent in certain quarters, the scope of legislation to make adjustments to continuous change is quite vast. It is true that there is a part of the Shariah which is immutable. But this part aside, there remains no less than nine-tenth of the Shariah which is a legitimate field for legislation. This gives an idea of the immense importance of the *ijmāʿ-ijtihād* process and, therefore, of legislation in Islamic society. This also provides an indication of the extent of flexibility, adaptability and progressiveness which are ingrained in the Shariah.

In order to illustrate further how immense flexibility and adjustability are mediated and ensured in the Islamic system of law, attention is drawn below to a number of ancillary and supplemental principles that have been in constant use by the jurists. These are drawn either from the Holy texts or from the legal maxims of the jurists. These principles and maxims provide a panoramic view of the Shariah's general spirit, liberality and sensitivity to human requirements and contingencies. An offhand selection of these principles and maxims is given here:

1. *Fulfil God's covenant, when you have made a covenant, and break not the oaths after they have been confirmed, and you have made God your surety; surely God knows the things you do* (al-Naḥl 16:91). This is an extremely wide and comprehensive command whose general applicability is quite vast. It enunciates two supreme values which must control and guide everything in the Islamic society. Imam Ibn al-Qayyim says in *al-Ṭuruq al-Ḥukmiyyah*: 'The purpose of God behind the Shariah is to establish justice among God's creatures. In whatever mode justice is established, that mode will be regarded as religion (*Dīn*) and not something contradictory to the religion' (p. 14).
2. *Allah wants ease and not hardship for you* (al-Baqarah 2:185).
3. *He has not laid down upon you any hardship in religion* (al-Ḥajj 22:78).
4. *Allah does not lay a responsibility on anyone beyond his capacity* (al-Baqarah 2:286).

5. Wisdom is the lost property of the believer, wherever he finds it, he has a better right to it (Tirmidhī).
6. Take that which is pure and clean and shun that which is impure and unclean.
7. Extreme necessity is exempted from the rules of the Shariah.
8. Extreme necessities make what is otherwise prohibited permissible.
9. It is undeniable that legal injunctions change with the changes introduced by time.
10. Injury is to be avoided as much as possible.
11. Do not cause that which is haram (prohibited) nor suffer that which is haram.
12. To eliminate a general haram, a specific haram may be tolerated.
13. There is no scope for futile and trivial things in the Shariah.
14. Haram should be avoided.
15. Neither do injustice nor suffer injustice.
16. Permission is the rule in all things.
17. Custom or usage is relied upon regarding that which is universally prevalent or acted upon in most matters.
18. Dislodging people from the things they are used to involves a great effort, disturbance and disorder.
19. Disorder is more severe than murder.
20. Benefit is the aim of the Lawgiver. All the Imams agree on this.

21. The responsibility imposed by the Shariah is conditional on possibility.
22. Where there is an undue harshness, it is proper to introduce ease.
23. The prevention of evil is given precedence over securing benefits.
24. My *ummah* is exempt from responsibility regarding committing an error, forgetting and being coerced to commit something wrong.

The above is just a random selection of a few verses from the Holy Qur'ān, extracts from Hadith and some well-known maxims. A plain reading of these can give one an idea of the great possibilities of flexibility in the Shariah. They are mentioned and relied upon in abundance in the works and treatises of the classical jurists. Along with *ijtihād* in particular, the principles of (i) *Istiḥsān*, (ii) *Maṣāliḥ Mursalah*, (iii) *Sadd al-Dharā'i'*, (iv) *'Urf* and *'Ādah* or custom and usage, (v) *'Umūm al-Balwā* and the disorderly state of the time create scope for an unusual degree of adaptability. Through the use of these instruments and maxims, a jurist has the power to do the following things: (i) to determine the priority or otherwise of the implementation of law; (ii) to make the law specific if it is general in its implications; (iii) to subject it to conditions if it is unconditional or absolute; (iv) to delimit it, if it is indefinite or wide; (v) to exclude from it certain things as exceptions; (vi) to add some conditions for the implementation of the law; (vii) to add some new features to the law for its implementation.

This bare description of different legitimate processes of law is an eloquent testimony of the extent of the role of human reason in applying the revealed and eternal principles to the concrete and mundane realities of our everyday world.

So far a description of the fundamentals of the Shariah has been given but only the theoretical aspect has been explored. However, one can get a much better and more accurate idea of the Shariah's capacity to adjust to all situations and circumstances by examining the practice and actual working of Islamic Law before its creativity was snuffed, leading to the petrifaction of the Islamic Law.

The ideal course for this purpose is to keep in view the practice of the Holy Prophet and that of the Rightly-guided Caliphs. Most of the practice of the Holy Prophet is recognised by the Holy Qur'ān itself as being an equivalent to Law. This is supported by the Qur'ān, *So accept whatever the Messenger gives you, and refrain from whatever he forbids you* (al-Ḥashr 59:7).

This does not apply to the sayings and opinions of the Companions of the Prophet. Nevertheless, they are regarded worthy of the greatest respect and attention. Their practices are rated as strong proofs. Furthermore, there is consensus that it is compulsory to follow whatever the first two caliphs had agreed upon.

One knows well that the *Ḥudūd* punishments are prescribed by Allah Almighty Himself in the Holy Qur'ān. Hence, there is apparently no scope for anyone to deviate from them. The importance attached to *Ḥudūd* is clear from a saying of ʿAlī Ibn Abī Ṭālib (may Allah be pleased with him), 'Establishing the *Ḥudūd* is of the same order as jihad in the way of God.' Nonetheless, one finds that the Holy Prophet (peace and blessings be upon him) himself prohibited the implementation of the *Ḥudūd* in wartime and on enemy soil (*al-Mishkāt, Bāb al-Sariqah*). According to another tradition, he said, 'Hands should not be cut during travel' (Abū Dawūd and al-Nasā'ī, *Bāb al-Sariqah*).

It would be impudent indeed to think that the Holy Prophet (peace and blessings be upon him) had deviated from or defied the words and commandment of God. On occasions like these, the Prophet (peace and blessings be upon him) acted under *Siyāsat al-Shariah* (Islamic Polity) on policy considerations to promote values and interests that are rated highest by Allah Almighty. Similarly, the Prophet (peace and blessings be upon him) was not rigid when making arrangements relating to conquered lands. He made different arrangements at different times and circumstances. Thus, we find that the practice of the Holy Prophet (peace and blessings be upon him) indicates that he applied tremendous flexibility to accommodate different dictates of time and circumstances. This tradition of the Prophet (peace and blessings be upon him) was continued by the Rightly-guided Caliphs.

Similarly, in early Islam, one comes across an extremely liberal and open-hearted approach, unhampered by narrow-mindedness and false pride, when seeking, learning and borrowing from others. This approach has been sanctified by such pronouncements as 'permission is the rule in all things.' In other words, everything is permitted unless it is specifically forbidden. 'Take that which is pure and clean and shun that which is impure and unclean.'; 'Wisdom is the lost property of the believer, wherever he finds it, he has a better right to it.' With a truly humanitarian attitude worthy of a universal religion meant for all mankind, knowledge is considered to be the common property of all mankind. However, in adopting the ways and customs of pre-Islamic times, or of other contemporary nations, the policy of Islam was always transmutation, rather than indiscriminate elimination. Yet, whatever was adopted or borrowed from others was impregnated with Islamic values and brought in line with Islamic norms and principles, after removing any objectionable or discordant elements.

The Holy Prophet himself set the trend in this context. At the Battle of the Ditch, he gave preference to the suggestion of Salmān al-Fārisī (may Allah be pleased with him), a Companion of Persian descent, over his own opinion in digging a defensive rampart around the town of Madinah. This practice was completely unknown to the Arabs but in common use among the Persians. Here, a Persian practice was unhesitatingly adopted, and even blessed with the approval of the Holy Prophet (peace be upon him) himself.

In the time of 'Umar ibn al-Khaṭṭāb, the boundaries of the Islamic state were expanded beyond the Hijaz and Arabia. Deeper contact was established with other highly developed cultures and the problems of the state and society became far more complex. As an enlightened and broad-minded administrator, Caliph 'Umar (may Allah be pleased with him) had no hesitation in adopting useful foreign ideas and practices after bringing them in conformity with Islamic values and principles.

(Reprinted with some modifications from *The Role of Judiciary and the Objective Resolution: A Plea for Reappraisal of Hakim Khan Case* by Sardar Sher Alam Khan. Islamabad: Institute of Policy Studies, 1994, pp. 68-85.)

# GLOSSARY

| | |
|---|---|
| *ʿĀdah*: | Habit, custom, usage. |
| *ʿAdl*: | Justice. |
| *Aḥkām*: | (sing. *Ḥukm*) rules, injunctions, prescriptions. |
| *Ākhirah:* | The Hereafter. |
| *Amānah*: | Trust. |
| *ʿAqā'id*: | Basic tenets of faith. |
| *ʿAql*: | Reason. One of the interest recognised as the purpose of the law by the Shariah. |
| *Bayʿ al-Istiṣnāʿ*: | The sale in the form of a contract for manufacture. |
| *Bayʿ al-Salam*: | A contract of goods with pre-payment. |
| *Burqa*: | Veil, full-length garment which covers women from head to foot, usually black in colour. |
| *Dalālāt*: | The different ways in which the meanings of texts to be understood. |
| *Dalālat al-Lafẓ*: | The implication of the text. |
| *Dalālat al-Naṣṣ*: | The implication of an explicit text of the Qur'ān or Sunnah. |

| | |
|---|---|
| *Dār al-ʿAhd*: | A country where Muslims live in contractual obligations with state. |
| *Dār al-Amān*: | Abode of peace. |
| *Dār al-Daʿwah*: | A country where Muslims can communicate the message of Islam. |
| *Dār al-Ḥarb*: | Enemy territory not under the jurisdiction of a Muslim state. |
| *Dār al-Islām*: | Territory under the jurisdiction of an Islamic state. |
| *Dār al-Kufr*: | Domain under the hegemony of the unbelievers. |
| *Ḍarūrah*: | (pl. ḍarūrāt) Necessity. |
| *Daʿwah:* | Communicating the message of Islam. |
| *Dīn*: | Religion, Way of Life. |
| *Dunyawī*: | Dealing with this world. |
| *Farḍ*: | Obligatory duty. |
| *Fasād al-Zamān*: | Prevalence of wide-spread corruption. |
| *Fatwā*: | (pl. *fatāwā)*: A formal legal opinion of a mufti that is, a qualified legal scholar. |
| *Fiqh:* | Islamic law and jurisprudence. |
| *Fiqh al-Aqalliyyāt* | Jurisprudence for Muslim minorities |
| *Fiṭrah:* | Primordial nature. The original state in which humans are created. |
| *Fuqahāʾ*: | (sing. *Faqīh*) Jurists. |
| *Ghalabat al-ẓann*: | Strong presumption. |
| *Ḥadd*: | (pl. Ḥudūd) Literal meaning is limit, boundary. A fixed penalty prescribed by Allah. |

| | |
|---|---|
| Hadith: | (pl. Hadiths) the sayings and actions of the Prophet as well as his tacit approval of actions. |
| *Ḥājah*: | (pl. Ḥājāt) Need, necessity. |
| Halal: | Lawful, permissible. |
| Haram: | Prohibited, unlawful. |
| *Ḥarb*: | War. |
| *Ḥayā'*: | Modesty, avoiding vanity. It is considered as part of faith |
| *Ḥifẓ*: | Protection. |
| Hijab: | Veil. Requirement for women to cover their head and body when they go out. Hijab is symbol of modesty, privacy and morality. |
| *Ḥikmah*: | Wisdom. The purpose or spirit of the law. |
| *Ḥukm Manṣūṣ*: | Textual Command. |
| *'Ibādah*: | (pl. *'Ibādāt*) Act of Worship. |
| *'Ibārat al-Naṣṣ*: | Explicit and literal meaning of the text. |
| *Ibqā'*: | Preservation. |
| *Iḍṭirār*: | Duress, necessity. |
| *Iḥsān:* | Excellence. It refers to the qualities of benevolence and good acts. To do something good and do it well. |
| *Ijmā'*: | Consensus of opinion of jurists. |
| *'Illah*: | An underlying legal cause of ruling. |
| Imam: | Leader. An honorific title used for Islamic scholars. |
| *Īmān:* | Faith. |

| | |
|---|---|
| *Ijtihād*: | Juristic reasoning by a suitably qualified scholar of Islamic jurisprudence based on Islamic legal sources. |
| *Infāq fī Sabīl Allāh*: | Spending in the way of Allah. |
| *Iqtiḍā' al-Naṣṣ*: | Required meaning of the text. |
| *Ishārat al-Naṣṣ*: | Alluded meaning, suggestion. |
| *Istidlāl*: | The literal meaning is to seek evidence (*dalīl*). In Islamic law, it's the pursuit of legal evidence by means of deduction. |
| *Istiḥsān*: | Juristic preference that is giving preference for the sake of human interests and objectives of Law over the result of *Qiyās*. |
| Jihād: | Utmost struggle, striving not synonymous to war. *Jihād bi'l-Nafs* is struggle against one's own desires and passions. *Jihād bi'l-Sayf* is struggle with sword. *Jihād fī Sabīl Allāh* is a struggle in the cause of Allah. |
| *Khalīfah*: | Vicegerent. |
| *Khuṭbah*: | Sermon given by an Imam during the Friday prayers as well as on festival of Eid Prayers and during Hajj. |
| *Makrūh*: | Undesirable, disapproved, dislike. |
| *Māl*: | Wealth. |
| *Mandūb*: | Acts recommended but not enjoined. |
| *Maqāṣid*: | (sing. *Maqṣad*) Literally it means objectives or purposes. The term is used for higher objectives of Islamic Law in general such as *Maqāṣid al-Shariah*. |

*Masāliḥ Mursalah*: Unrestricted interests also referred to public interests. Although not explicitly identified by the Qur'ān or Sunnah they deal with issues which arise in human society, for example setting up of administrative offices, road maintenance and waste disposal,

*Muʿāmalāt*: Social transactions.

*Mubāḥ*: Permitted, legally indifferent acts.

*Mu'min*: A believer, a synonym for a Muslim.

*Mustaḥabb:* Recommended.

*Nafs*: Soul.

*Nasl*: Lineage, progeny.

*Naṣṣ:* Text; definitive implication of the text that the Qur'ān or hadith.\

*Al-Qawāʿid al-Kullīyah*: Universal Maxims.

*Qiṣāṣ*: Retaliation for loss of life or limb.

*Qitāl*: Fighting, war.

*Qaṭʿī*: Definite.

*Qiyās*: Analogical deduction or basing legal ruling on a previous ruling about a similar case.

*Qiyās Khafī*: Latent analogy.

*Ra'y*: Personal opinion.

*Ribā*: interest and usury.

*Risālah*: Messengership, Prophethood.

*Ṣadaqah*: Charity, benevolent acts for which there is reward from Allah.

| | |
|---|---|
| *Sadd al-Dharāʾiʿ*: | The prohibition of evasive legal device, or anything leading to which is forbidden. |
| *Ṣalāh*: | Ritual prayers. |
| *Shakk*: | Doubt. |
| Shariah: | The Islamic legal code which embraces all aspects of life. |
| *Sunnah*: | The precedents laid down by the Prophet (peace and blessings be upon him) to be followed as binding law. |
| *Tadrīj*: | gradual procession. |
| *Taḥsīniyyāṭ*: | Complementary comforts. |
| *Takāful*: | social welfare and support. |
| *Taqlīd*: | Strict following of one school of *fiqh*. |
| *Taqwā*: | Piety or fear of Allah. This requires one to remain God-conscious. |
| *Tawḥīd*: | Oneness of God. |
| *Tayammum*: | Dry ablution. Wiping of the face and hands with clean earth or dust for achieving ritual purity. |
| *Taʿzīr*: | Discretionary penalties. |
| *Tazkiyah*: | Self-purification. |
| *Ulamāʾ*: | (sing. *ʿĀlim*) Scholars, jurists. |
| *Ummah* | The Muslim nation. |
| *Ummatan Wasaṭan*: | The community of the middle-way. |
| *ʿUmum al-Balwā*: | A general necessity. |
| *ʿUrf*: | Custom, usage. |
| *Uṣūl*: | Principles of *Fiqh*, Jurisprudence. |
| *Wahm*: | Whim. |

| | |
|---|---|
| *Wājib*: | Obligatory. |
| *Wuḍū'*: | Ablution required before performing prayers. |
| *Yaqīn*: | Certainty. |
| *Zakah*: | Its literal meaning is to purify. Believers are required to pay a calculated amount of money from their savings every year. |
| *Ẓann*: | Presumption. |

# BIBLIOGRAPHY


Khurshid Ahmad (ed.): Chirāgh-e-Rah, Islamī Qānūn Number. , Vol. 12 (6-7) 1958. 2Vols.

Taha Jabir Alalwani: Towards a Fiqh for Minorities: Some Basic Reflections (London: International Institute of Islamic Thought, 2010. Revised ed.)

Muhammad Asad: The Principles of State and Government in Islam (Berkeley, CA.: University of California Press, 1961.

Jamaluddin 'Atiyah: Fiqh al-Aqalliyyāt: Ta'āruf, Tajziyah awr Ḥall [Jurisprudence of Minorities: Introduction, Analysis and Solution] (New Delhi: Ifa Publications, 2012).

————: Islamī Sharī'at kā 'Umumī Naẓriyah [General View of Islamic *Sharī''ah*]. (New Delhi: Islamic Fiqh Academy, 1993).

'Abdur Rahman I. Doi: Shariah: The Islamic Law (London: TaHa Publications, 1984).

————: Women in Shariah (London: TaHa Publishers, 1989).

Ghair Muslim Mumālik me Ābād Muslamānū ke khuch Aham Masā'al [Some Important Problems of Muslims Living in Non-Muslim Countries]. (New Delhi: Ifa Publications, 2010.Pp. 53-68)

Encyclopaedia Britannica http://www.britannica.com/science/mortality-demography,accessed 27 September 2017.

Encyclopaedia Britannica 1984 vol.7 p.163, http://www.britannica.com/search?query=Rate+of+divorce+in+ western+society. Accessed 27 September 2017

Kate Figes: Our Cheating Hearts: Love and Loyalty, Lust and Lies. (London: Virago, 2013.)

Mahmud Ahmad Ghazi: ʿAsr-e-Ḥaḍir aur Sharīʿat-e-Islāmī (Islamabad: Institute of Policy Studies, 2009).

————: Muḥaḍrāt-e-Fiqh (Lahore: Al-Faisal Nāsharān, 2005).

————: Muḥaḍrāt-e-Sharīʿat (Lahore: Al-Faisal Nāsharān, 2009).

Alan Godlas (comp.): The Five Universal Maxims of Islamic Law. (al-Qawāʿid al-Kulliyah al-Khams) http://islam.uga.edu/law_maxims.html Accessed 27 September 2017.

Wael B. Hallaq: Sharīʿa: Theory, Practice, Transformation Cambridge: Cambridge University Press, 2009.

Wael Hamza: Sharīʿah: Bringing Values to Our Lives: Characteristics of Shariʿah.

https://lecturesnthoughts.wordpress.com/category/islam/understanding/ Accessed 27 September 2017

Zoya Hasan and Ritu Menon: Unequal Citizens: A Study of Muslim Women in India (New Delhi: Oxford University Press, 2006).

Yusuf Abbas Hashmi: *Shariah, Ummah and Khilāfah*. (Karachi: University of Karachi, 1987).

Murad Hofmann: Islam the Alternative (Reading: Garnet Publishing, 1993).

Howell, Nicole: A Link Between Single Parent Families and Crime.

Ed.D. Dissertations Paper 79. School of Graduate and Continuing Studies, Olivet Nazarene University, Bourbonnais, Illinois 2015.

http://digitalcommons.olivet.edu/cgi/viewcontent.cgi?article=1078&context=edd_diss. Accessed 27 September 2017

Hymowitz, Kay: The Real, Complex Connection Between Single-Parent Families and Crime. The Atlantic, December 3, 2012.

https://www.theatlantic.com/sexes/archive/2012/12/the-real-complex-connection-between-single-parent-families-and-crime/265860/. Accessed 27 September 2017

Muhammad al-Ṭāhir Ibn Āshūr: *Treatise on Maqāṣid al-Shariah* (London: The International Institute of Islamic Thought. 2006).

Muhammad Iqbal: The Reconstruction of the Religious Thought in Islam (Lahore, 1930.)

Zafar Iqbal: Justice: Islamic and Western Perspectives (Markfield, Leics. : The Islamic Foundation, 2007).

Sultan Ahmed Islahi: Musalmān Aqlliyatun kā Maṭlūba Kirdār [The Desired Role of Muslim Minorities] (Azamgarh: Fikr-o-Āgahi, 1988).

Mohammad Hashim Kamali: The Legal Maxims of Islamic Law (London: Association of Muslim Lawyers). http://www.sunnah.org/fiqh/usul/Kamali Qawaid al-Fiqh.pdf Accessed 27 September 2017

————: Maqāṣid Al-Shariah Made Simple: (London; The International Institute of Islamic Thought, 2008).

————: Shariah Law: An Introduction (Oxford: Oneworld Publications, 2008).

Wahiduddin Khan: Women in Islamic Shariah (New Delhi: The Islamic Centre, 1995).

Andrew F. March: Islam and Liberal Citizenship: The searching of an Overlapping Consensus (Oxford: Oxford University Press, 2009).

Sayyid Abul A'lā Mawdūdī: Towards Understanding the Qur'ān: abridged version of Tafhīm al-Qur'ān; translated and edited by Zafar Ishaq Ansari (Markfield, Leics. : The Islamic Foundation, 2006).

————: The Islamic Law and Constitution; translated and edited by Khurshid Ahmad. Lahore: Islamic Publications, 2005.

———— : Islāmī Riyāsat (Lahore: Islamic Publications. Ltd. 1962).

Khurram Murad: Shariah: The Way to God( Leicester: The Islamic Foundation, 1981).

————: Shariah: The Way of Justice (Leicester: The Islamic Foundation, 1981).

Muhammad Tahir Mansoori: Shariah Maxims: Modern Applications in Islamic Finance(Islamabad: Shariah Academy, International Islamic University, 2007).

Mallika B. Mistry and John Dayal: http://scroll.in/article/ 669083/ muslim-women-and-the-surprising-facts-about-polygamy-in-india. Accessed 27 September 2017.

Syed Abul Hasan Ali Nadwi: Ijtimā'ī Ijtihād(New Delhi: Ifa Publications, 2010).

Shaikh-ul-Islam Ibn Taimiyah: Life and Achievements (Leicester: UK Islamic Academy, 2005).

Tārīkh-e-Daw'at wa 'Azīmat (Karachi: Majlis Nashrīyāt-e-Islam, 1976).

Imran Ahsan Khan Nyazee: Theories of Islamic Law: The Methodology of Ijtihad (Islamabad: Islamic Research Institute, International Islamic University, 1995).

Yusuf Al-Qaradawi: The Lawful and the Prohibited in Islam (Indianapolis: American Trust Publications, [1960]).

Said Ramadan: Islamic Law: Its Scope and Equity 2nd ed.(1970).

Ahmad Al-Raysuni: Imam al-Shāṭibī's Theory of the Higher Objectives and Intents of Islamic Law (Kuala Lumpur: The International Institute of Islamic Thought [and] Islamic Book Trust, 2006)

Aslan, Reza: No od but God: The Origins, Evolution, and Future of Islamg. (London: Random House, 2011).

Adil Salahi: Pioneers of Islamic Scholarship (Markfield, leics.: The Islamic Foundation, 2006).

Abdur Rashid Siddiqui: Qur'ānic Keywords: A Reference Guide (Markfield, Leics, :The Islamic Foundation, 2008).

Mohammad Najatuallah Siddiqui: Maqāṣid-e-Sharīʿat (Islamabad: Idārah Taḥqīqāt-e-Islāmī, 2009)

Salahuddin Sultan: *Fiqh Al-Aqalliyyāt: Tāʿaruf, Uṣūl awr Taṭbīq* [Jurisprudence of Minorities: Introduction, Principles and Application] (New Delhi: Ifa Publications, 2012).

Shāh Walīullāh: The Conclusive Argument from God [The translation of Ḥujjat al-Bāligha] by Marcia K. Hermansen. (Islamabad: Islamic Research Institute, 2003).

# INDEX